...ND YOUR
...REAM JOB

...ries and proven strategies for
...a job you love

WADE

...AROLE ANN RICE

Marshall Cavendish
Business

Copyright © 2009 Sarah Wade and Carole Ann Rice

First published in 2009 and reprinted in 2010 by
An imprint of Marshall Cavendish International

PO Box 65829
London EC1P 1NY
United Kingdom

and

1 New Industrial Road
Singapore 536196
genrefsales@sg.marshallcavendish.com
www.marshallcavendish.com/genref

Marshall Cavendish is a trademark of Times Publishing Limited

Other Marshall Cavendish offices:
Marshall Cavendish International (Asia) Private Limited, 1 New Industrial Road, Singapore 536196 ·
Marshall Cavendish Corporation. 99 White Plains Road, Tarrytown NY 10591-9001, USA · Marshall
Cavendish International (Thailand) Co Ltd. 253 Asoke, 12th Floor, Sukhumvit 21 Road, Klongtoey Nua,
Wattana, Bangkok 10110, Thailand · Marshall Cavendish (Malaysia) Sdn Bhd, Times Subang, Lot 46,
Subang Hi-Tech Industrial Park, Batu Tiga, 40000 Shah Alam, Selangor Darul Ehsan, Malaysia

A CIP record for this book is available from the British Library

ISBN-13 978-1-905736-47-8
ISBN-10 1-905736-47-9

Printed and bound in Great Britain by
TJ International Ltd, Padstow, Cornwall

For my mum
– Sarah

In gratitude to my husband Patrick and my beautiful children Phoebe and Raphael for blessing me with my dream job
– Carole Ann

CONTENTS

FOREWORD

I love stories. A well-told story is extremely satisfying. A true story, especially one with a happy ending against the odds, can be enthralling.

Recently, I have been hunting out people with great stories to tell about career change. People who have made the decision to improve their lives, to really fulfil their potential, to find something they feel passionate about, and make a go of it.

I wanted to pass their stories on. I told a friend and career coach and she said, "Sarah, you're right. These are great stories. Why don't you write them down, make them into a book?" I rolled my eyes, and laughed. What I was actually thinking was, "Me? I can't write a book!" But then I thought, these people had the courage to take an important step and change their lives. Why can't I do something similar, and write a book about these inspirational people for all those who have yet to take that step? I don't have to invent the plot. They've done it for me!

I visited bookshops and looked around at the shelves groaning with new books. I was daunted. But then I began to think, if they can do it, so can I.

After all, I knew the subject struck a chord. Everyone knows someone who loves or hates their job.

So I tracked down some of those people, and soon found some more, and I asked them to describe individual journeys. Their searching, struggling and achievement. They seemed only too happy to talk, and I reached a stage where I couldn't wait to talk to the next new person. Like any passion, it's become an addiction.

Every story I heard (even those for which there was finally no space) inspired me and, for that reason, informed this book. I hope they inspire you too.

Sarah Wade

Everyone at some point or other has had the nightmare job. The one with the psycho boss, the gossipy back-stabbers and endless hours of tedium draining your life away.

I know I've had a few in my time, from selling door to door on commission only, to working in an environment so macho that it made All-Black rugby team changing rooms (post victory match!) look like a beauty parlour.

So I retrained and found my métier. Now, as a coach, I am acutely tuned into the pain and despair behind my clients' declaration: "I simply do not know what I want to do."

I can hear in their voices and see in their slump-shouldered demeanour that their vampire vocation has sucked dry their lifeblood and spirit.

Being in a job you dislike will undermine your confidence and your sense of self.

But it doesn't have to be that way. Culturally we think work is something we have to endure, not enjoy. We moan about our energy levels, the commute, the people we work with and the work itself.

Given that we live in an age where broadband companies compete to save you seconds in connecting to the Internet and that fast-food outlets can deliver meals in under a minute, then why would we waste years of our lives doing work we don't like?

It usually all comes down to one little word – fear.

That is why, throughout this book, I provide real coaching tools for those wobbly moments. I aim to keep you going, offering support, cheering you on from the sidelines just as I would my own clients. Sometimes the journey is not as painful or as difficult as you think it will be. Sometimes it's harder.

But one thing I do know for sure – it's a journey infinitely worth taking.

Carole Ann Rice

CHAPTER 1

THE RUT

> **"**For me the most important thing in my life is love … If you are not in love with your job, you must change your job.**"**

José Mourinho[1]

At her leaving do, under a tree in Regent's Park one glorious Friday evening, management assistant Sheila raised a glass and said farewell to her colleagues. She concluded the evening with the following words:

> Before I go, just a few reminders. The wineglasses are behind Mike's door. The stationery cupboard is that big container right in the middle of the office. With stationery. The toner – which comes with simple replacement instructions – is in the cupboard marked "Toner". And the tea and coffee machine is right in front of you. The people have been brilliant. But let's not beat about the bush – it's been s***.

And that final word neatly summarized the low points and utter tedium experienced in Sheila's working life over the previous four and a half years. It conveyed exactly why she was leaving for a different kind of job in a different kind of organization.

To counter the boredom in her day job, Sheila ran her own annual art fair and had another weekend job with an organization promoting reading with libraries around the UK. She had to have something in her life that tapped into her passion for literature and the arts. Eventually she was recommended for a job as an arts events producer, attended an interview and got it. That is exactly what this book is about – making change, in order to get to where you want, and need, to be.

OPERATION GET ME OUT OF HERE

Can you imagine what it would be like to enjoy what you do? Engaged, driven and so excited by the prospect of the coming week you can't sleep – from excitement rather than dread? This is the feeling described repeatedly by the interviewees. One person commented that nowadays, in spite of the fatigue, they are up and ready to go at the crack of dawn.

This book is based on interviews I (Sarah) made with a set of people around the world who love their jobs. There is nothing more infectious than hearing people talk about work that they love.

But that's not enough, is it? What people really want to know is how those people got there. How did *she* work out what she wanted to do with her life? How, after twenty years in the same office, did *he* go from a dud job that he hated to the dream job that turned his life around?

If you are someone who feels stuck in a rut, it's quite likely that your friends, partners and work colleagues are tired of it, just as much as you are. So this book assumes that you're someone who not only feels stuck, but is in need of ideas and practical suggestions for making successful change *right now*.

My research shows that most people find that the major obstacles to making change are not knowing what they really want to do and, even if they do, not knowing how to make it a reality. The interviewees in this book prove that it is possible to overcome the obstacles to change. They overcame the stagnation and found the nerve to leave dull jobs to go and hunt for a better one. They knew that there had to be something more. This book examines the process they underwent and details both the successes and, in some cases, the long-drawn-out struggles.

They all made choices, both big and small, that changed their lives. The kinds of choices they made are ones that anyone who wants change will need to make.

HOW TO USE THIS BOOK

For anyone who's looking for improvement in their working life, it's important to be able to see change immediately. So each chapter contains a "career coaching boot camp" section by my co-author, one of the UK's leading coaches, Carole Ann Rice. This section is designed as a workbook from which you can plan, plot and devise goals and strategies to help you move from baby steps to giant leaps.

Coaching is an action-based, goal-focused and transformational process that gets the individual unstuck from bad habits, negative beliefs or behaviours. Be it stultifying procrastination or sheer fear which prevents the individual from moving on, coaching can powerfully help unravel the often self-imposed obstacles standing in the way of success.

Carole Ann recommends that you keep a coaching journal throughout this process in which you can monitor your thoughts, fears, breakthroughs and insights. It is by gaining awareness of these things that a new perspective develops, energy is released and clarity forms.

"Coaching is a journey that doesn't happen overnight," says Carole Ann. "But with honesty, questioning and finding ways to explore and enjoy your quest for a new job, a path does start to open up. I ask that everyone embarks upon the process with courage, hope and curiosity, and to accept that despair and frustration are the occasional, and natural, by-products of a new adventure. I see people through this sort of transition every day, and the dips are a perfectly normal part of the experience, along with the highs that come from seeing your goal and getting nearer to it. If you see the lows as part of the process too (and realize that you can learn the most from them), they will not have you surrendering at the first knockback and throwing in the towel. You will read in these stories how many people benefited from their searches not taking them where they thought they would and how disappointments and rejections proved to be godsends in hindsight. And when you truly 'get' that you have nothing to fear but fear itself, opportunity and possibility present themselves in extraordinary ways."

THE BRUTAL FACTS

"You have to really, really want it," one interviewee said to me. "You only get one chance. You can't keep on reinventing yourself, starting at the bottom and working your way up."

But I include stories from people who didn't know what they "really, really" wanted to do for a living. They left their jobs to find out, and some of them had a host of jobs before they hit the right one. But while they may not always have known the exact shape of their future role, most of them knew their strengths, their talents and the area they were attracted to. That is something you will need to know, or get to know – even if you've never known it before. The Career Coaching notes will help you with this.

IF YOU DON'T LIKE YOUR JOB – YOU'RE NOT ON YOUR OWN

Nearly one in three of us claims to be unhappy at work. Indeed, British workers spend an average 25 minutes each day chatting to friends, daydreaming, web-surfing and looking for other jobs, and this costs their employers £40 million a year.[2]

So why do people stay in jobs they say they can't stick? A recent survey claims that 36% of us are too tired to do anything but slump on the sofa after a day at work.[3]

In which case, how are we supposed to muster up the strength and energy to change an unrewarding job? You know you don't have the dream job, but it's easier to stay put if you don't know what you really want to do. There isn't enough time as it is, let alone the time to conjure up an escape plan and put it into practice.

Your first decision is to agree that things cannot continue as they are.

IF YOU DON'T LIKE YOUR JOB, WHY DON'T YOU LEAVE?

When I showed the manuscript of this book to a publisher and asked for some feedback, he said quite bluntly, "I don't get it. If you don't like your job, you leave." I was taken aback. But he went on, "I've always enjoyed my job and made sure I've done work I like. I used to be an academic and I enjoyed that too, but I was surrounded by plenty of people who didn't. They just stayed and complained but I never understood it."

For some people it's that simple – if you aren't happy, leave. But for many people it isn't. Financial risk, not knowing what to do, not having the right skills for a new career – all are reasons for staying put (more in Chapter 3). When unsure about which path to take, people tend to find something to blame – laziness, procrastination, being too attached to the comfort zone, being too old, being too young, it being too late.

But there is one simple thing that is behind all of these things that stop us leading the lives we know will make our heart sing – FEAR.

HOW LONG WILL IT TAKE?

The stories I have collected demonstrate repeatedly that the length of time for change can vary, and it is not uncommon for the process to take several years. Often, interviewees had been thinking about change for long periods, and in one particular case for twenty years! Undoubtedly, it always takes longer than you think. But in the interim, get things under way immediately to ensure you have everything in place to create that opportunity or to be ready for it when it comes your way. Taking small, achievable steps now will enable a bigger change in the future.

GETTING STARTED

Commit to change – right now. Do something differently in your daily routine. Why? Breaking old habits will bring new thoughts. New thoughts will bring freshness and much-needed energy. Take a different route to work, read a different magazine, listen to something new.

What one small, achievable thing can you set in motion that will make a difference to you? Anything from fifteen minutes in the fresh air at lunchtime to sorting out your wardrobe or the unopened post. Start small but commit to something NOW that makes life feel better immediately.

COUNTDOWN TO YOUR DREAM JOB
Carole Ann's career coaching boot camp

Just as if I was coaching my clients I have designed these coaching tips to fit in with the process you may experience when embarking on your dream job journey. Euphoria can easily morph into misery as you ride the highs and lows of hope and disappointment. This is completely normal, and all through the book I request that you don't give up and that you stick with it.

In parts you will find the tips thought-provoking and challenging, and I ask that you have the courage to be as honest with yourself as you can possibly be. Do keep a journal to monitor your pathway through the process, and keep an open mind so that you can make the most of what you learn along the way.

Whether it's baby steps or giant leaps, go at the pace that suits you.

These tips work, but, like anything else to do with personal development, whether it's weight loss or taking up exercise, you get out only what you are prepared to put in. Overnight change is rare but not unheard of, so be prepared to give it time too.

CAROLE ANN'S ACTION PLAN

1 The first stage of the book is to move out of stagnation. Buy a lovely thick notebook in which to write down your thoughts. This will be your coaching journal and will record your progress. In time, you may not even recognize the person who wrote what they did on page 1.

2 As you go about your daily life over the next week, start to be aware of what you enjoy, what motivates you, and what feels effortless. Keep these thoughts in your head and you *will* start to notice things that give you that "ah-ha" feeling.

3 "Get" that you deserve to do something you love. Look at those limiting beliefs that could be holding you back – beliefs such as:

> I don't deserve to have …
>
> I can't do this because …
>
> How on the earth will I …?
>
> My father said be an accountant as it's safe, but I'll never …

Reject them!

4 Write down what it is costing you to *not* do what would make your heart sing. Tiredness, resentment, depression, impotency, jealousy, self-esteem problems. Be very truthful.

5 Put despair on hold and start to believe this can happen for you and allow the positivity and bliss of that thought to teleport you. Doubt, fear and cynicism will tie stones to your dreams and sink them.

CHAPTER 2

A MENTAL SHIFT
TO THE NEW YOU

66 I really think if people are positive about life and everything they do, they're far more likely to succeed than those people who are negative about life. I'm a great believer in saying 'yes', rather than 'no', to everything. **99**

Richard Branson[1]

If you're currently trapped at your desk and hating every minute of your time there, you're probably not the nicest or easiest person to be working with right now. You need to be transported to a much happier place.

Therefore, changing your circumstances must be your priority. The responsibility for your career rests with you. People will want to help you achieve your potential, but all the time and energy you hoped your preoccupied manager was going to invest in you, *you* need to invest in you. And to get in the right frame of mind you need to ditch any things in life that drag you down.

That includes all those people who see their cups as empty – regardless of their permanent jobs, boyfriends/girlfriends, promotions and pay rises. Their approach to life is all part of the rut you are leaving behind. You're homing in on people whose cups are overflowing. You'll recognize them immediately – energized and energizing people, passionate people with a zest for life, people with stacks of friends and a packed social calendar. Their outlook is infectious and addictive. Eventually it is *their* conversation you will seek out rather than the comfort of cynical, negative chat. If you think positively you will behave positively, and everyone wants to work with positive people.

Not convinced? Give it a whirl and see. This book will introduce you to such people. Patrick didn't start out as positive. In fact he was a seething ball of negativity. Once he ditched the negative, he and his life were transformed.

* DREAM JOBBER

Patrick

Age: 48

Was: Insurance clerk, UK

Now: Trainee wine merchant, UK

Key to success: Worked with his passions

Passions: Wine, books, history, cricket

Patrick and I met in the lounge of the Savoy. Sitting under bright chandeliers and near the pianist, surrounded by lone business diners, we drank our carefully selected wine.

This was the hotel to which both Monet and Whistler came in the 1880s to draw and paint views of the Thames. Patrick chose the venue because he is fascinated by history, old buildings and facts. After a two-year hunt and several jobs, Patrick thinks he's found the path to his dream job. By day he indulges his love of books and history by working in his local prison library, and by night he learns about wine at a nearby college. Patrick has worked out exactly what he needs for job satisfaction.

Go back a few years, and there was nothing positive in Patrick's working life. He was stuck in an insurance office feeling totally trapped and unable to move on. To one way of thinking, he had it all – a safe job, a regular income, a house and a wife. Nothing to complain about there. Except he did complain, because he was bored to tears and overwhelmed by inertia. He oozed bile and whinged every day until eventually it made him ill. Any of this sound familiar?

How on earth had he ended up stuck in something so far removed from any of his real interests?

He had started out doing a stint teaching English in Crete, and then joined his father in the family wine business. He had no long-term aim, but he enjoyed the shop work and found the physical elements of handling the stock and stacking shelves more enjoyable than he expected. And he loved the product.

> It was great fun really, learning about wine and meeting people, and I also travelled to Europe as part of the job. Unfortunately, after three years we could no longer compete with the supermarkets or cope with the rent increases, and the business went bankrupt. I panicked and immediately joined a temping agency. This led to work at the insurance company who, after a short placement, offered me full-time employment. It was the easiest and safest choice to accept and stay on.

Patrick settled at the insurance office – indeed, it was a permanent job he could easily have stayed in for life. But he *hated* it.

> I worked in an open plan office with 40 people. Each day the prospect really depressed me. The routine paperwork, dealing with customer complaints about mistakes in other departments, the stifling bureaucracy, the buck-passing.

In spite of all this, he accepted the misery because of the regular income.

> I didn't talk about my passions or interests in the workplace. I adopted this fixed role and personality at work. I was earning a living, but not with people who had the same interests as me. I could talk about what we did, money and so on, but nothing that was "me". Over time I became increasingly aware of the split between the "work me" and the "outside work me". I would say I was giving only about 20% of myself at work.

Patrick continued trudging along. He tried looking for other work locally, but just saw similar types of jobs on offer for less money, and there was nothing that he really wanted to do.

> The options seemed limited in my area, in addition to which I had no real pressures in my life to force me to make changes, so I stayed in this rut. Pressure would have helped, an objective would have helped. I didn't know what I wanted. I had some vague ideas, but nothing concrete. I was very much in a comfort zone, and it was easier to stay put than instigate the turbulence of change.

Ah, the old "comfort zone"! But far from being comfortable, Patrick appeared to be on "autopilot", tolerating rather than enjoying life. There are consequences to living a life where Patrick was sometimes giving only 20% of himself to his job. Indeed, settling for less took its toll on Patrick when he developed migraines and stomach upsets, and went sick. With hindsight he believes that the real root of the problem was "a combination of stress and boredom".

> I hated talking about my job because I saw myself as "just a clerical worker". But at that time, because I couldn't see any alternatives, I felt my future lay within the four walls of the company. I applied for a position as a financial adviser in another department. It was a sideways move, but I thought it was a role more suited to my abilities. I was offered the job, but within two weeks I realised it was the worst thing I could have done. I was assigned a trainer who was aggressive, had zero faith in my abilities and went out of his way to undermine me. I went from being very frustrated to feeling even worse about my work and underwent a total loss of confidence.

Getting an even more appalling job might have seemed disastrous for Patrick, but, in fact, it was the *best* thing that could have happened to him. This new "all-time low" proved the catalyst for positive change. By making a move, any move, it stopped the stagnation and ultimately generated a crisis and turning point for Patrick.

In hindsight, people do sometimes come to feel grateful for a worsening in their work world. "If he hadn't been such a chronic boss," one interviewee said to me, "I wouldn't have been so determined to find something else." The zone was no longer comfortable. The same applied to Patrick: "If it hadn't got so much worse," he says, "I would probably still be there now. I carried on whinging. I was sick of it and so was everyone else. I reached a breaking point which forced me to confront change."

THE SHIFT

Up to this point Patrick felt he had no choices about work. So what changed to make him feel that there had to be more than this?

> At this time I felt I couldn't leave my job because I needed money and I continued to see no opportunities anywhere else. However, I felt I did have a choice about what I did beyond the office: I could eat and watch TV, or I could eat and watch TV and do something constructive. I chose the latter. It was a fundamental decision and I began to think about what I could do.

A chink of light penetrated his negative thought processes, for there was hope – and there was a choice. Instead of focusing on what he couldn't change, he started small and tackled what was within his control. He looked at the possibilities outside work and stopped dwelling on all the negatives consuming him during the day. He reached a stage where even he recognized the need to get something positive into his life.

> Building on my previous experience in the wine trade, I decided to qualify in wine tasting. My first step to change was to take advantage of flexitime at work and I came in early so I could leave by 4 p.m. That small shift made a considerable difference to me. I made the time to attend a wine course and I found my passion for it just took

over. After completing the evening classes I went on to devise my own wine appreciation course. I planned the course structure and content and then I took it to my local college and said I wanted to teach it. I wanted to show people that the choices they had in a restaurant about food also applied to wine. They thought it was a great idea and I set up and taught the course for a year. It did wonders for my self-esteem, and my confidence soared. I had initiated this, it was all my own work and it felt totally liberating. I could look at myself differently when I felt typecast at work. *I learnt that when you do what you are passionate about, you are transformed.*

Patrick wasn't ever going to be able to leave his insurance job until he had regained his confidence and rediscovered some positives in life. By building up skills on the side, and having fun at the same time, Patrick could begin to see possibilities. Before, he couldn't see beyond the four walls of the building he worked in. He woke up to the realization that there were more ways to earn a living than what was on offer in the local papers.

I came to the realization that I could earn this sort of crap money somewhere else. *That* wasn't even a reason to stay. By doing the wine course I had learnt a lot about myself and my capabilities. I began to think about how I could make this work for me. What other courses could I do? Where did I want to work? In the future, I knew I couldn't work in an office. I had enjoyed working with groups of people on the wine course. I didn't want to teach, but what else could I do that enabled me to talk to people about things that interested me? Over a week it began to make sense. At first I was swayed by blind panic and I thought I would do *anything*. Later I took a more considered approach and decided to pursue one or two things, which made it much easier.

So, over a week Patrick's life began to make sense. A *week*! Some of us have been at this for years! Still, it's good to know that a picture of the future can emerge quite quickly. Although, in many cases, it may not be realized for some time.

To broaden his options and research other possibilities, Patrick also began to train as a London tour guide. It drew on his love of history and required many of the same skills used in his wine-tasting classes: performing, research, knowledge and an ability to communicate to groups of people. By pursuing his interests outside work, he finally felt confident enough that he could earn some sort of living from other sources. Patrick lost his fear and finally took the plunge and handed in his notice.

Following a period of soul-searching and shopping around for the right career, Patrick's love of wine has re-emerged and he's signed up for a part-time degree. As he says, "If you have a passion, you often come back to it." While looking around he pursued his instincts and tried things out: he did a stint tour guiding and worked in a winery, a bookshop and a library. Patrick has transformed from being someone stuck and blinkered in their outlook to a person unfazed and capable of quickly finding new work. He now wants to fulfil his potential, not waste life moaning about a job he hates. But it hasn't been clear and straightforward for him. In the background there are still yearnings for a career in librarianship or a second-hand bookshop, but it's the wine trade which gets him more excited than anything else. His wife even bought him some vines for his birthday to get him started. His current job working in the local prison library funds his degree. But to make this retraining financially viable he has had to make sacrifices.

> Money-wise I'm thinking like a student again, and am making small adjustments to make money go farther. No longer spending £4 a day on lunch, which works out over eleven months as a third of my tuition fees for a full year! And my travel expenses have now gone from £600 per year to nothing at all! Also, buying wine in France

saves money and I'm not going to give up that essential! Ideally I need a job back in wine. Initial thoughts are New Zealand, working during their harvest. I am excited about the challenge of being something of a scientist (it is a science degree, after all), working outside, learning new skills (driving a tractor!) and being part of the renaissance of English wine. Probably an element of the rose-tinted spectacles here! A week in Burgundy, seeing the harvest in action and seeing some wonderful scenery, has been an inspiration and confirmation of my hopes and ambitions. So, I'm making a living, paying my share of the bills and looking forward to the future.

Ironically, in one sense Patrick has come full circle, both in what he wants to do and where he's living. He initially saw where he lived as being the source of his limited working life but, after a period of time acquiring jobs and self-confidence, he has been able to return to the same area with a clearer idea of what he wants and what he has to offer.

It's hard to think that Patrick was ever "stuck in a rut". Since making that initial mental shift towards something positive, if anything irks him nowadays he no longer endures it, but moves on. He is someone confident enough to take risks and he is full of energy and motivation. He ended temping jobs quite swiftly when employers didn't keep their word or he started to get dragged down by office politics. Having lost six valuable years at the insurance company, Patrick has a renewed sense of urgency about his future. But he's finally hunted down what he really wants – a career in wine.

PATRICK'S ADVICE

1   Give yourself a break from misery. Spend more time doing things you find interesting. Attach yourself to things you enjoy. Your spirits will be lifted and you'll get your energy back.

2   Find whatever it is you want to do and find the right time, but do it as soon as you can. That course, travel, time out from work – just *do it*. After all, what is the worst that can happen? There is always work, we can all do things.

3   If you feel trapped economically, as I did, look at how you utilize your leisure time. How much time can you devote realistically to your passion – there's no excuse. The easiest thing is to be lazy. I was a prime candidate, but even I eventually reached a point where the rut and all the negativity that came with it became plain boring. Find the thing that makes you happy, excited, animated and alive! The thing you *need to do*.

4   I kept a journal. It was something I could look at to track the tiny, sometimes minuscule, progress I had made. I could see the move from the rut to something more positive. It's hard to believe I thought I was better off where I was working in insurance doing a job I hated. It's terrible in retrospect that I convinced myself there was nothing I could do. I didn't do anything until I reached breaking point. Having left the insurance office, I simply pursued my interests and, from there, began to work out the future.

> **TOP TIP**   You learn nothing in the comfort zone. Aim to feel butterflies in your stomach once a week.

COUNTDOWN TO YOUR DREAM JOB
Carole Ann's career coaching boot camp

AUTOPILOT PITFALL

We all have coping mechanisms, whether it's comfort eating after a crisis or reaching for the Chardonnay after a gruelling day at work; these are little habits we employ to ease the pressure valve. But on the whole, short of meditation or some sort of exercise, few coping mechanisms are sustainable.

Patrick confesses to giving just 20% of himself to his job when it was at its worst for him. He was on autopilot, living for the evenings, weekends or payday. Huge chunks of his life, time, energy and soul were suspended in a horrible grey ennui of gloom. Life was on hold. Sure, it helped him get through the mind-numbing tedium. But what were the consequences? He mentioned being depressed, isolated, irritable with colleagues, and I'm sure his home life wasn't a barrel of laughs after a week of that either.

When we tolerate things they drain our energy and then other areas start to decline. The impact is far reaching and can affect our moods, our perspectives on life, our health and our happiness.

What are you tolerating in your life this moment? Whether it's the killer commute or the tight shoes you wear to work each day, write a list of things you are tolerating and decide to zap them.

When we are fully using our strengths or being valued and respected for what we do, we feel energized and useful. We feel compelled to do what is required of us because we are doing and being our best. This feeling of motivation comes naturally and isn't forced or false. We are being real, present in the moment and not treading water and wasting our lives.

Imagine that?

CAROLE ANN'S ACTION PLAN

1 Avoid "energy Hoovers" (negative people) who will want to do down your vision and may feel threatened by it.

2 If you find yourself becoming anxious, cynical or despairing, move on to something that fills you with joy – music, a good friend, being creative.

3 Remember, what you focus on expands – keep positive.

4 Write a list of things in the past that you are proud of, difficult things you've overcome, and get that YOU CAN DO THIS.

5 You're right to want something better. You don't have to suffer in your job or be in pain in order to feel you are achieving something. What would your life look like if you loved what you did each day and you lived with meaning and purpose? You do have a choice. What would need to change in your life so that you could fully honour your potential? Allow yourself to dream. Put yourself in the ideal job. What does it look like?

6 Listen to the whispers. What did you do in childhood that you adored? What do you love now? What feels easy and effortless and fills you with joy that you hadn't in a million years dreamt you could get paid for? Even the most off the wall pleasures need consideration.

CHAPTER 3

IDENTIFYING AND GETTING OVER OBSTACLES

"I just thought, well, I want to write, and I wrote the book, and what is the worst that can happen? It gets turned down by every publisher in Britain, big deal.**"**

J. K. Rowling[1]

What are the main obstacles for people achieving what they really want to achieve? What prevents them sending the resignation email, applying for jobs, writing that book, making that phone call and taking the first step?

In a recent survey, the following were cited as reasons for not being able to leave a job:[2]

1   "The possible drop in salary" (70%)

2   "My family's needs" (37%)

3   "I feel I am too old to change career" (27%)

4   "The cost of retraining for something"/"I don't have the right qualifications for what I really want to do" (23%)

5   "Apathy" (17%)

6   "The possible drop in status" (14%)

7   "The stress of learning new skills" (10%)

8   "The area I want to enter is too competitive" (8%)

THE DROP IN SALARY

It's listed here as the main obstacle to changing career. So, what can you do to get yourself into a healthier financial position so you have some options?

Financial adviser Ann Watcyn Pugh fervently believes that if you are proactive about your finances you do not have to stop doing things.

But if you want to continue with the double espressos and lavish nights out, you'll need to put some effort in.

Here are seven key action points suggested by Ann for getting your finances in order so that you do have a choice about changing your future. "And you only have to do it once," she says. "Then you can concentrate on your new career."

1 REVIEW YOUR MORTGAGE/RENT

You could move it to another lender for a better rate or make it a fixed rate for a couple of years so you know exactly what the monthly payment will be for a while – and particularly during your period of transformation. It is worth taking independent advice on this. A small charge paid here could save you a fortune. Why a fixed rate? In preparation for making change, getting a fixed financial foundation makes a huge psychological difference. Quite often people have never considered a fixed-rate mortgage. It's the biggest loan you'll take out in your life, and people often view banks and building societies as figures of authority, so they don't feel they are in a position to change anything. But you are. If you're renting, you might have the flexibility of downsizing while you get your change under way.

2 MAKE A FINANCIAL PLAN

If you're hoping to make a career change, get a plan of your finances in place. Don't bury your head in the sand and ignore it. Take professional advice and make a realistic assessment of your financial situation. What's the least amount of money you can afford to live on?

3 GET RID OF CREDIT CARD DEBT

Get rid of high interest rate charges on credit card debt. Transfer your credit card debt to a 0% deal (they are often interest free for a year). It gives you time and the head-space to clear it. Check that there is no exorbitant transfer fee before you dive in. And look for cards that give cashback rather than points.

4 GET YOUR MONEY TO WORK FOR YOU

Check that your bank account and savings are earning the highest rates of interest. You will find that Internet accounts usually pay the most, because the bank is carrying out less administration. Rates are published in the weekend press.

5 ORGANIZE YOUR ACCOUNTS – START BEING FINANCIALLY DISCIPLINED

Set up a separate account from which all your bills are paid. Have one direct debit from your current account to cover the cost each month (and even a little more if you can afford to save some). Such practice instils financial discipline and ring-fences money for paying the bills. Certain costs, such as mobile phone charges, will be unknown, but paying the essential basic bills is the priority.

6 BOOST YOUR INCOME

If you have a spare room, could you rent it out? If you live in a city, why not have a part-time lodger? Many people rent a room from Monday to Friday, then return to their families for the weekend. Also, look at comparison websites – check that you are paying the lowest rate for your gas, electricity, car insurance, buildings and contents home insurance, etc.

7 SAVE WHILE IN WORK

Save for retraining and prepare for an ad hoc income.

 TOP TIP If you're earning a lot of money – start saving. If you're not, you're free to earn rubbish money elsewhere doing something that suits you.

What about the other obstacles cited above as reasons for not changing your job? Do any of these resonate with you?

MY FAMILY'S NEEDS

Get your friends or partner to support you. They'd rather know someone happy and healthy than be around someone who is miserable and unbearable. Get them on board and engage them in the plan. Can you negotiate three hours on a Saturday to do your research, make notes, meet people? At this stage you need to beg and borrow the time. You need to be responsibly selfish for the greater good.

I FEEL I AM TOO OLD TO CHANGE ...

Provided your new profession does not rely on manual labour or excessive stamina, there is no reason why you shouldn't start to follow your dream. With age comes wisdom and patience. The forties are the new thirties, the sixties the new fifties – the ageing population has much more stamina, worldliness and greater consumer power than it's ever had. The grey pound rocks!

THE COST OF RETRAINING FOR SOMETHING/ I DON'T HAVE THE RIGHT QUALIFICATIONS

If you were buying a shop or a café or any new business it would cost a lot more than buying a college or university course. Investing in training is like buying yourself a new future; the money you spend is buying you a new profession and a business opportunity. This will be your greatest investment and asset.

Find out whether your current employer might part-finance your tuition. Have you investigated a grant? Would a loan be feasible if you came up with a sensible business plan?

Are you 100% sure you need to spend a lot to train? Many leading entrepreneurs, like Karen Brady and Richard Branson, have had no formal training. Never negate how far passion, know-how, networking, volunteering and charm can take you.

APATHY

What exactly is draining your energy? When we sit procrastinating, there is usually an underlying fear that needs addressing. Ask yourself what you are scared of and use this as a starting point for a new awareness.

THE POSSIBLE DROP IN STATUS

What does status mean to you? Does it validate you, does it make you who you are? What does success mean to you? The material trappings of wealth, or living life with meaning and purpose?

Status anxiety maketh a modern blight on the land. When we worry about not looking good or keeping up with celebrities we are on a one-way ticket to misery. Happiness, passion, waking up each day wanting to leap into work – these are priceless when compared to chasing the golden egg through years of boredom, fatigue and depression, too burnt out to enjoy your weekends or your retirement.

Nobody says treading the path towards doing what you love is easy. But, with courage and persistence, it could be a journey of great possibility and satisfaction. Stay as you are and what do you have? *Guaranteed* unhappiness. And a lifetime of "what ifs".

Besides, who says there will be a guaranteed drop in status?

THE STRESS OF LEARNING NEW SKILLS

Toddlers can work computers and pensioners are uniting on social networking sites. So you *can* teach old dogs and young pups new tricks. Why make learning stressful? It could be thrilling to learn to master something new. It could be an intellectual challenge and an exciting new way of connecting with like-minded people. Have you considered the satisfaction levels of learning something new?

There are so many ways to learn now – correspondence courses, residential courses, workshops, work experience, local college evening classes. There must be one method with your name on it. Talk to someone who is doing what you wish you could and see whether there are alternative routes to get to your goal.

THE AREA I WANT TO WORK IN IS TOO COMPETITIVE

Every profession and business sector is competitive. Competition is healthy. Learn from what your competitors do and then be creative about how you can do it differently and better. Think about what your offer will be, how you compare and how you intend to add value. No one else is *you*, so use what you have to create a competitive edge. Go the extra mile, provide a unique service, develop a media profile and trust in yourself.

Developing a niche can make you stand out from the crowd. What's your USP? How will you do things differently? Why would people use you?

Be your message and deliver it with style. Be the 'brand' by living and working within your values and your passion. Never let the flame of what drives you flicker. Let it burn brightly and let your market see your love and energy for what you do. Pretty soon you will *be* the competition!

 Don't wait for things to be perfect – they never will be.

In the process of researching this book, the only regrets I ever heard were from those who hadn't made change sooner. They admitted, in hindsight, to making excuses – often due to fear. But what if you accept you're bound to be nervous? That you'll get things wrong, be rejected and need to take big risks? If you acknowledge and accept fear, and then get on with it and tackle the obstacles – what happens? Well. Let's see. Take the case of …

✱ DREAM JOBBER

Jenni

Age: 42

Was: University teacher, UK

Now: Jacked it all in to find dream job

Key to success: Regained responsibility

Passion: Is still looking

Jenni has yet to find what she wants to do. But she has at least taken one, decisive step along the road to finding out.

In spite of having outgrown her eighteen-year job as an EFL teacher in London, Jenni stayed put. Worried by the usual obstacles – other people's opinions, the loss of status, the loss of money, the not knowing – she became stuck. Until suddenly, quite out of character, with nothing else to go to and despite all the perceived hurdles, she handed in her notice, "just like that".

Several tipping points (health, work conditions, poor management, being overlooked for promotion) generated a sudden clarity, and she knew she had to go. "What are you waiting for?" she said to herself as her mouse hovered over the resignation email. "When I sent it I felt fantastic!" I spoke to her a few weeks after she'd handed in her notice. "*I'm* really well," she said, "it's just everybody else."

In the aftermath, she found a new job looking after other people's children. The minute people knew she was available, ad hoc work came her way. With no regular income, the key at this stage, she felt, was not to be choosy.

The biggest stumbling block to my leaving was other people's ideas of what I ought to be doing. The things I *could* do (cleaning, cooking, looking after kids) were not regarded as desirable occupations. I struggled with the idea of losing the status I felt I had by being a teacher in a university. We are defined by our jobs, but when I was teaching I was bored and I didn't want to talk about mine.

I hate the fact people in the UK ask the question *"What do you do?"* (Why don't they ask "How do you enjoy yourself? What music do you like?") I watch people on the school run do a double-take when they find out I gave up a teaching job in a university to child-mind. It gives me a thrill every time I say it!

How was Jenni eventually able to overcome the long list of obstacles keeping her chained to the same old routine and hand in her notice as a qualified teacher? If we go back and find out more about her teaching career, we discover several contributing factors.

As she began to think about her future, Jenni noted the gradual deterioration of an older colleague in the staffroom.

With every passing year I would see her energy evaporating. She was just getting older and holding out for retirement. I would see myself in her shoes in years to come and became acutely aware how easily time was passing. Her working life reflected back on my own. I'd ended up in teaching by default because I didn't know what I wanted to do. I enjoyed it 70 to 80% of the time – which is not bad going. I appreciated its flexibility and it took me away from an office existence in front of a screen. But I'd never thought "this is the job I want to do". It had always been in my head that I would get out.

Jenni had enjoyed teaching, but it never felt like her vocation. After seven years doing the same thing she started to think about making a change, and although she had liked the job for much of the time, she uses the phrase "get out" when talking about leaving – as if she was trapped or imprisoned. She reached a stage where she felt deflated by the poor conditions. In reality, she was working really very hard, for precious little money. After eighteen years she still didn't have a continuing contract.

> So I applied for a permanent job within the university and I didn't get it and it crystallized my thoughts. Getting the job would have provided the contract and benefits that had always eluded me. Would I have been able to give that up to pursue a passion? When I didn't get that job, I analysed my situation: I was exhausted, I had no contract and was still being paid an hourly rate.

Not getting the job she thought she deserved was her wake-up call. It was one of those low moments in the change process which proved a revelation.

> I realized I needed to pave my own way. I could no longer rely on others to do it. I needed to start valuing myself and recognizing my own worth. That thought gave me a perspective on myself. Here I was, being paid by the hour, scrabbling over scraps of work, and being made to feel grateful. When I finally broached the subject with colleagues I realized these thoughts weren't only going on in *my* head, it wasn't "just me". So I kept my job, but simultaneously applied to another college for an additional part-time job with a proper, permanent contract. I got one. At last! Then, after all that, I didn't like anything about the new job. I cried every morning before school and I handed in my notice after only one term. This was unlike me and was a huge deal. I was always loyal, and leaving was a new experience. I agonized over writing my resignation email, worrying about the exact wording.

Pursuing an additional job at a different college to track down what she thought she wanted – a permanent contract – was a fundamental step for Jenni and it marked the end of her long stagnation. It was only by making that shift and experimenting somewhere new that Jenni acquired much-needed information. A permanent contract was not necessarily going to provide the fulfilment she was looking for, but it kick-started some movement and enabled her ultimately to move on. "If I hadn't done the job at the other college, which I hated, I wouldn't have done anything. Why is it we don't do anything until things just get so awful? People are just too scared to do anything until we reach that point."

I really empathized with Jenni's story of struggle, lack of direction, fear of the unknown. She battled on in her search, curious and game enough to try out different things.

> Opposite the station on my way to work, there was a small deli, selling soups and cakes. I said to myself, "Just explore something – anything!" There was a notice in the window advertising for staff and, as I'm a bit of a foodie, I phoned up and expressed an interest. I met the owners and was offered twenty hours a week and I worked there in conjunction with my job at the university. Suddenly everything became manageable because I had something other than teaching in my life.

Jenni took an absolutely vital step by putting something positive into her working life. It revitalized her. The sense of possibility, freshness and confidence flooded back in to counterbalance what drained her back in the staffroom.

> I baked cakes and worked in the shop for seven months and it was great. It acknowledged my other skills and I was in a different environment with different people. The pay was low and I was exhausted, but it was in a totally different way to teaching. It was hard work, but it was energizing. I'd had these ideas for years and I told myself, "Go and do it!" I needed to stop romanticizing jobs which I knew nothing about.

Jenni stopped living in her head and "made it real". She gained valuable knowledge about herself and a different kind of environment by doing something new. And she began to get practice in the art of resigning!

> I reached a stage at the café where I felt I'd done this now. I looked at it financially and it made sense to do more work at the university. I emailed the shop owners when I was off for a few days and it was easy. I was beginning to get over my phobia of handing in my notice and feeling disloyal. When I realized running a shop was not exactly what I wanted to do, I started to imagine what would happen next. I thought I'd do "something else" and that would become my main thing. But that didn't happen. Then I thought my career would be a two-lane manoeuvre doing two jobs simultaneously, but they'd eventually turn into a single lane.
>
> As it turned out, I ended up on a cliff edge! I reached a stage where I realized I just wasn't going to know what "it" is. This elusive career change continued to evade me. We think so much about destinations, doing this or doing that. It's never about the ride to get there. I told myself, I can do things to earn money. I can clean, cook, look after children, rent out a bedroom in my flat. I can earn money. I can survive and I can pay my way.

The moment of realization came after a few days' sick leave. A stressful, hard-working summer with long hours had resulted in illness. Jenni ended up doing parts of the job she'd been overlooked for, and not getting paid for it. Stress-related symptoms began to re-emerge. She knew it was because of the job, and if she didn't make a move, under these conditions, the problem would recur. She didn't want the rest of her life blighted by ill health.

From that moment on it was simply a question of when she was going to resign. Although now more familiar with the process of leaving, she still thought about it for a week. She had made the decision, but found she was scared about having made it. She dragged this out, agonizing over the decision and giving herself the chance to change her mind.

But deep down she knew she'd made up her mind, there was no going back, and she needed to inform the university so they could find a replacement. The indecision took up a lot of energy, which she found symptomatic of the whole experience. "All this energy was being used up and drained from me. Just imagine what I could achieve if I invested all this wasted energy in something positive and worthwhile."

You may think that all Jenni did was hand in her notice. But for anyone used to eighteen years of a regular income and a daily structure, giving it all up with nothing to go to is a huge and, some may say, ill-advised step. What was the reaction to such an abrupt departure?

> People's reactions to my leaving have been very interesting. Some friends were shocked. And my parents were anxious because, for them, it's all about your job. Some teachers knew, but didn't say anything. But one colleague took me aside and said, "You don't know what you're going to do? Fantastic!" And my Aunt Daisy, who's 80, said, "Not happy in your job? Don't stay there! Take your time, but sort yourself out." She'd worked in a factory, but her life was her family and everything outside. She wasn't defined by what she did all day. I really needed to hear that encouragement.

Jenni knows that if she had continued to wait for a revelation about her role in life, she'd still be in the classroom. She'd waited eighteen years and taken periods of time out to travel in the hope something would "come to her". But it never did. She eventually recognized that continuing in the same rut would never get the doors open to something new. So, even though she didn't know where she was going, she jumped ship anyway. She rationalized her situation, was realistic about what she could do and created the space to do some exploring to find something different, whatever it turned out to be. She found the courage to overcome the fear of risk that had kept her chained to a job she had outgrown. She found the courage to leave a job with status, to do a job that has none. But the fact is, Jenni finds it more worthwhile. She grew tired enough of the draining situation she was in, and lost the fear of leaving it. She set off to hunt down her new future. "Things come up if you let them. I realized the fear was in my head and I am perfectly capable of doing other things."

Seven months on from leaving and Jenni has new plans for her future. Having had some space to think and reflect, she's also had room to do other things. A stint working in a community vegetable garden started to tick all the right boxes. She's in the process of planning her next move, establishing contacts and preparing to get a foothold out of the city. "Living in the city, I now realize, is part of the problem." There are plans to get voluntary gardening work to build up experience and qualifications, working at a garden in a heritage centre, and the return of an old idea – running a bed and breakfast in the country. Now flooded with ideas, she feels the next stage is setting out the process to get there, and from that establishing what's truly realistic.

JENNI'S ADVICE

1   What enabled me to start the process of change was to do something different.

2   Rather than just chucking in your job, before you leave you need to have a clear idea of who you are. So, try something else, go part-time, take a month off, have a long holiday. Look around. It's not until you do something different that you'll re-energize yourself and be able to put your current job into perspective.

3   You may come to realize that a lot of the obstacles or problems are in your head. I began to realize that I did have choices. I had some

savings, I could do other things, I could get a lodger if I had to. I began to have faith in myself that I would be OK.

Jenni found the courage to take the first, decisive step into the unknown. Georgina went farther.

✳ DREAM JOBBER

Georgina

Age: 35

Was: Housewife, Australia

Now: Successful businesswoman, Australia

Key to success: Regained responsibility

Passions: Music, teaching, children, life

Georgina is Australian. When I first spoke to her on the phone at her home in Melbourne she sounded bubbly and enthusiastic. But her life hasn't always been that rosy. The day her husband walked out, her life changed "in an hour". The obstacles that confronted her were enormous. And yet, through a series of transformations, she turned herself from unambitious housewife into successful businesswoman.

> I sit here now with a flourishing business, a business that I love with a passion, and I earn more than I ever dreamt of. Even though I sometimes get tired and narky, I still spend most of my day smiling.

A key to Georgina's eventual success has been knowing her passions and being stubborn enough to pursue them. Her one-and-only aim as a teenager was to move to Ireland. So she saved her money and, at eighteen, in spite of having no contacts and against all the advice, bought an air ticket to Dublin, a cold, wet country with few jobs. She lived there for four years and the experience she gained was invaluable. She fell in love with the country, its culture and, above all, the music. "Parents and children sang together, and being able to play an instrument was just part of the culture. This didn't exist back home." By working as a nanny she was able to stay on for four years. But, after a great and illuminating time, an eventual yearning for a support network of family and friends brought her back home to Melbourne. She carried with her life-changing memories of an Irish culture where music was simply a way of being. It provided the blueprint for her future.

Back in Australia, she settled into her life, finding her feet after four years away. She started working as a nanny and eventually felt confident enough to embrace the education she'd walked away from at the age of eighteen. She now knew she wanted to study music. Her job funded the training. During this time she also met her future husband.

A year and a half into her course she spotted an advertisement that ran: *"Do you like working with children? Are you musical?"*

> The advert was so small I could easily have missed it, but as soon as I saw it I said, "That's me!" I love children and I love music. I called the number and got an interview with a no-nonsense, straight-talking entrepreneur called Jen. She was a formidable woman – brusque, but warm and funny. A typical teacher. She gave me a very short music test, she asked me to sing, and she hired me on the spot.

The owner had ambitious plans for her new company, which was in its infancy, and she threw the new recruits in at the deep end, teaching them hundreds of songs over just one weekend. Georgina was terrified ("I thought I was going to be sick!"), but she stuck with it, and as her confidence grew, so did her love for the job. Soon she took on a company franchise herself.

But her life as a businesswoman was short lived. She was married now, and the greater demands of her husband's work meant that she decided to give it all up, sell the franchise, follow him back to Europe, and choose to become a full-time housewife. At this point she didn't have a career bone in her body. Her husband was an accountant, he looked after all the finances and she just went along with it. She took this period away from home as an opportunity to have a rest from music. "And I was exhausted, vocally I was worn out, I saw it as a break and I put music to one side."

But after three years they were back in Australia and Georgina revived her part-time work with the music teaching company.

> My boss, the owner, kept urging me to buy a franchise, but I was still in housewife mode. Then my husband walked out the door and I never saw him again.

As you can imagine, this dramatic change in Georgina's circumstances left her shell-shocked. She was an emotional wreck, overwhelmed by the obstacles that suddenly faced her, including the need to pay the rent. And yet her transformation from passive dependant to independent high-flyer began the moment her marriage ended.

> I was earning very little money and I was utterly broken hearted and stricken with grief. My whole life completely collapsed and I cried in the toilets between every class for about a year! Until then I had no idea the human heart could hurt that much. But I also had no idea of the healing power of music and children.

THE NEW GEORGINA

As a consequence of her change in circumstances, Georgina had to quickly evolve into someone different.

I learnt that you grow so fast in a break-up, you almost explode. You are a different person from week to week. As well as the emotional aspects, I had to learn new skills to get by. It was a huge period of growth. Divorces are tricky and very technical to understand. After ten years in a relationship, it forced me to relearn independence. I had to do things my husband had always taken care of. I had always avoided the responsibility for them. I had to pay the solicitor, understand the terminology and terms and conditions of the divorce settlement, sort out the finances and set up new bank accounts, refinance and buy a new house. All of this was transforming. These were all things I could do, but I didn't know it. This was the biggest learning curve I underwent and it certainly paved the way for buying a new franchise and running my own successful business.

THE CAN'T DO LIST

Momentous, often traumatic events like redundancy, a significant birthday, a bereavement or illness can help clarify what is important in life, and what we want.

For Georgina, divorce boiled down to survival. Amid the emotional turmoil, she needed to deal with the practical daily basics, such as having enough money to pay the rent. Through sheer necessity she set about addressing her obstacles, and she did it in a rather brilliant way. Instead of setting up a 'To Do' list she set up a 'Can't Do' list.

I remember specifically that I sat down and made a list of everything I couldn't do. All these obstacles that I had: I didn't understand finance, I'd become frightened of driving in the city centre, I didn't know how to take responsibility for the car, I couldn't use a PC.

I turned it around. I read up about finance, bought books, got the *Financial Times* and learnt about stocks and shares. Every Sunday I would choose a new highway I hadn't been on before and would drive on it. I learnt reverse parking, parallel parking and hook turns, and the day I made it on to the Westgate Bridge I sat screaming in the car with delight because I couldn't believe I'd found it, let alone was driving on it! The woman in the car behind me clearly thought I was insane. Now I drive all the time. You can learn anything if you want to and now I am constantly reskilling and looking for new challenges. This year, for example, I want to learn all the handyman know-how – brackets, taps, changing a washer.

STANDING ON A CLIFF EDGE

Georgina was at a low ebb in life and lacking self-confidence, but she was lucky enough to have a mentor. Mentors can prove a very useful asset, providing advice, experience, contacts or opportunities. Georgina's mentor was her employer, Jen, who took her out to dinner and forced her to confront her new situation.

> After my marriage ended, in her usual straight-talking way, Jen asked, "So what are you going to do?" Well, I cried a lot, but Jen had a way of making you laugh even when things looked so bleak! She was the salt of the earth, who believed in women looking after themselves. (Something I was still learning to do.) I felt as though I was standing on a cliff edge and I had this choice, to jump and see what happens, or to stay put. I said to myself, "What's the worst that could happen?" You simply have to be brave sometimes. Jen was the pivot who tipped me over the edge – in a good way! At the end of dinner I took a complete leap of faith and bought a new franchise. I had absolutely no idea if I would make enough money to support myself, but I had moved in with my parents and they also encouraged me to give it a go.

Convinced that her life was at rock bottom, Georgina took a risk. She felt she had nothing left to lose. She describes this particular evening as "lifesaving" and the turning point that enabled her to move on.

You have no idea how much I think of that evening. As I sit here now with a successful business that I love with a passion, earning more than I ever dreamt I would. I bought an apartment that I love so much and I have the life I always dreamt of. I will still live with my parents for another year, but that is an emotional decision rather than a financial one.

Georgina's entire focus and energy went into getting her new business on its feet. She had run a franchise for a short time previously, but now there was no longer a second income as a security blanket. Financially this business had to work.

THE CHALLENGE

She had a constant fear of the unknown and the worry that the business would fail.

When I filled in the first three-month spreadsheet I cried, because I had only earned $300 per week. It was obvious to me that this *wasn't* going to work and what was I going to do? I phoned a friend in hysterics, and she promptly told me to get over it otherwise she'd come over and kill me herself!

She was forced to learn new business skills quickly, but was daunted by the administration and the spreadsheets.

I was pretty hopeless at first and would fill in the financial stuff incorrectly. But I had gained confidence, I knew I was intelligent and – hell, whatever the problem was, I'd somehow manage to work it out! Each time I made a mistake I just got my head down and gave it a go. When you're pushed into a corner, you can work it out. When you need to pay the rent, you do it somehow! I got shouted at a lot in the beginning. But I was still getting over the divorce and my brain was not working properly. It took longer for me, I was slow at learning and I needed a lot of support. I stuffed up the money but I was always honest with head office, and as a result I have maintained a good relationship and they provide me with the support I need. In business, your reputation goes before you.

She knew she had to be good at dealing with the customers.

I needed bums on the floor! Mums are busy people with little time. I needed to be sensitive to their needs. Some mums are hesitant, but I'm good now at knowing how to sell the business and understanding the clientele. Maintaining those relationships leads to a lot of repeat business, which is really important. But I also feel you have to enjoy the business in order to sell it. I'm not the type of person who could convince others unless I felt passionately about what I do myself. Mums have a high "nonsense radar", they don't have time for it. Children are honest and mums recognize honesty and I need to deliver.

Her strategy was to give herself incentives and rewards.

I put all my energy into the business to get it on its feet. I knew it would take about two years. I stuck my goal of 150 clients on the bathroom mirror to motivate me every day. But I made it fun and rewarded myself when I reached my targets with a facial, champagne or a weekend away. I wanted to ensure I didn't beat myself up and had plenty of incentives to keep going and enjoy the process. Someone advised me that it's really important to celebrate the successes with a new business, otherwise you'll forget what you have achieved when the chips are down.

HER MENTOR'S LEGACY

Georgina's inspirational mentor, Jen, fell ill and died suddenly. But her business continues to thrive and her words of encouragement still fuel Georgina's motivation.

That small enterprise is now a Melbourne institution and we have many franchises in the area. On the day Jen died, I went to see her with a large group of her teachers. Something changed me that day for ever. I had always felt that what I did wasn't good enough because I didn't have a university degree. Jen had spent the last twenty years giving music to children and as I watched her dying I found myself thinking that if I even give a tenth of that to children, as she did, I will die happy. Her death made me see what a precious and important job our teachers do. For me, music is lifeblood for the soul. I get to fill them with the joy of pure sound and harmony. When I'm teaching, something takes over. When I'm teaching, I'm at my happiest and I can't believe I get paid to do it.

Georgina has her dream job: running a successful business doing what she loves. And she did it by establishing her passions in life and pursuing them. When life threw things at her she kept going – only just, but with support from friends and family she didn't give up and go under. Sometimes in life, in order to make change, bravery and taking a risk are necessary. "If you don't try," says Georgina, "you'll never know."

She had a crucial meeting with her accountant recently to discuss the company's financial situation and assess whether she could continue. "I was sick beforehand, I was so nervous. I was worried I would lose my flat and didn't know what else I could do. When he told me how much I'd earned after tax, it was more than I'd ever dreamt of. Not only could I afford to live, I could afford to buy a flat. "I love you," I shouted at my bewildered accountant; "this is the best day ever!"

GEORGINA'S ADVICE

1   Change doesn't have to be sudden and dramatic as it ended up being for me. If I'd had a choice I would have made change more gradually rather than plummeting head first into a new business.

2   If you're stuck in something you don't like, instead of walking away immediately, why not go four days a week at first? Think calmly and work out what is feasible for you. Look at the skills you have got. There are always skills you can take with you.

3   If you're angry about being in a rut, you can galvanize that anger and use it as an impetus for moving forward.

COUNTDOWN TO YOUR DREAM JOB
Carole Ann's career coaching boot camp

Jenni was wise to note that society is at fault for routinely asking of us "what do we do?" instead of "what do we enjoy?" Notice how the whole prospect of facing change becomes less onerous when we ask ourselves what it might be that excites us.

Considering we have finite years of work, why shouldn't the journey be one of joy and adventure and not just duty and safety?

When it comes to choice, most people vote for unhappiness over uncertainty. The odds are poor. The unknown may well deliver your heart's desire, but it involves risk. The former will almost 100% deliver every time.

What freezes us into the "safe" place of miserable familiarity is that our brains fast-track to the worst-case scenario where horror stories of failure, rejection and catastrophe play out in the IMAX cinema of our mind and glue us to the spot.

But in Georgina's story one of the worst-case scenarios did happen. Her husband walked out, leaving her ill equipped with essential life skills like being able to drive or fix the plumbing, and she faced a major life downturn. She didn't even know not only whether she could pay the rent but how you physically do it.

Even in this situation, perhaps the worst she'd ever found herself in, her survival instincts kicked in and she learnt new skills and tuned into a neglected wellspring of tenacity, courage and fortitude.

If you faced your worst-case scenario, think of all that could be done to pull you through. What might be the hidden benefits and possible positive outcomes of such an experience? What could you learn?

CAROLE ANN'S ACTION PLAN

1 Assess what is stopping you from pursuing change.

2 If you really want some changes, then make the time and space. If you feel you are "working in overwhelm", remember that even this is a choice. Working in overwhelm is when you feel powerless, there are not enough hours in the day, you can hardly breathe with all the things you have to do. It feels as though external circumstances have conspired against you. Be responsible for that overwhelm. What options can you create now and what can you simplify or say no to? What will give you the space you need? Stop digging and find an escape route.

3 It's time to stop beating yourself up. Give yourself a break and rewrite your negative beliefs. If you are believing "I am useless, I will fail", reprogramme your thoughts with a more nurturing mantra – e.g. "I am enough and I will succeed" – act "as if" it were true, and pretty soon you will believe and those around you will too.

4 Find time to keep a "Big Me Up" journal. Write down everything you've ever achieved from being a loyal friend to successes at school or work. Ask your friends what your strengths are and start to gather positive evidence about yourself that you can refer to when you are feeling low. Then believe it.

5 In preparation for change, can you start saving? What sacrifices are you prepared to make to get to the bigger picture? Can you increase income by selling stuff on eBay or at car boot sales? Make savings by using recycling websites and borrow the books or equipment you may need for your new career.

6 Don't struggle. How can you make this process easy, fun and enjoyable? If you were merely being curious in investigating change, would this take the despair out of the situation?

CHAPTER 4

WHAT IS IT YOU WANT? WHAT ARE YOUR VALUES?

"Your work is going to fill a large part of your life, and the only way to be truly satisfied is to do what you believe is great work, and the only way to do great work is to love what you do. If you haven't found it yet, keep looking, and don't settle. As with all matters of the heart, you'll know when you find it.**"**

Steve Jobs, Apple[1]

In his speech to Stanford College graduates in 2005, Steve Jobs described the moment when he dropped out of college. It enabled him to stop going to what he didn't enjoy and start dropping in on the classes that really appealed to him – calligraphy, for a start. At that time, he said, it had no practical application and it made no sense to do it other than to satisfy his own interest and curiosity. Ten years later it formed the basis of the Apple Macintosh fonts and typography.

In his speech Jobs talks about the importance of "connecting the dots".

> Of course it was impossible to connect the dots looking forward when I was in college, but it was very, very clear looking backwards ten years later ... You can only connect them looking backwards, so you have to trust that the dots will somehow connect in your future. You have to trust in something – your gut, destiny, life, karma, whatever – because believing that the dots will connect down the road will give you the confidence to follow your heart, even when it leads you off the well-worn path, and that will make all the difference.

Jobs dropped out to search for something that appealed to him. He wasn't sure what it was, and in his pursuit he didn't know how it would all come together. He just pursued what interested him, and went with it in the hope that something would emerge. His is an astounding success story. But, as well as highs, it also features plenty of real lows.

YOUR VALUES

Searching for your true vocation can be helped by establishing your values. Often we work in organizations that don't marry with them. When you work in an environment where you feel upset, anxious or unable to fit in, it could be that the organization is in complete conflict with your own values. This leads to unhappiness. It doesn't mean to say, however, that the organization is wrong in its values, merely that you are struggling to relate to them.

If you discover what your values are and then work within them, you will operate at your very best, and you will be at your most energized. Working with your values makes you feel great. That's what is happening when people say "I'm tired, but I'm happy tired." They don't mind the long hours if they are doing something that they love.

A "VALUES" EXERCISE

Let me present you with an exercise to help identify *your* values, the things that you like to do naturally, the things that fire you up, the things that help you feel most yourself.

1   Identify and recall five moments over the last few weeks when you felt truly happy and at peace. Then try to formulate a simple way of expressing this as a value.

My moments, for example, include:

●   **Visiting an inspiring art gallery and wishing I could paint**

My value: *Being inspired*

I need to be inspired on a regular basis. It tells me that working solo in a grim open-plan office without sharing ideas wouldn't work for me because it deprives me of my need to be and feel inspired. When looking for the ideal working environment, factor in such knowledge.

- **Talking to a new interviewee**

My value: *Adventure and discovery – in myself and other people*

I need to be experiencing and learning something new on a regular basis and I love to hear stories from others doing the same. Creating this book provides me with exactly that.

- **Cycling to work**

My value: *Freedom and autonomy*

Avoiding the gridlock gives me a real feeling of independence. Being an assistant to someone else doesn't feel right. I need autonomy and the chance to run my own projects, organize my own workload.

- **Making and baking**

My value: *Creativity*

It comes in many forms. For myself, I appreciate creativity in others but I also need a creative outlet.

2   Having singled out the things in life that you really enjoy most, the things that gives you a deep sense of fulfilment, then ask yourself

- **What does this list of values tell me about myself?**

If you like playing football every Saturday, does that mean you like routine? Or does it mean you like being with people? Or is it teamwork? Or is it merely exercise?

- **Now, what does it say about me in the context of the world of work?**

Do you need to be out there in charge, or do you like being in the background holding everything together? Do you need deadlines? Do you need people around you or do you need peace and quiet? (The kind of environment you work in can be as important as the work that you do.)

3   Write down your top five values and keep them with you. Find ways to work within your values for maximum happiness. If, for example, you decide responsibility, freedom and independence are key values, being stuck at a desk with a control-freak boss isn't going to suit you.

 Have your values at the heart of what you do.

GETTING ENJOYMENT INTO YOUR LIFE

Make time in your life for those elements you now know you like! Of course it's obvious, but do you make time for something positive you know you enjoy each week? Writing? Playing music? Running? Socializing?

If creativity emerges as something that's important to you but is currently neglected, consider how you might regularly bring it into your life. It might be through art classes or taking up the saxophone. Or it might be through cooking, entertaining, travelling, improving your beautiful home, devising a party invitation.

What's the right way for you to express your creativity? At work it might be in problem-solving, getting the best out of someone, motivating a team. Or it might be creative use of lunch hours or screen breaks.

BALANCE

Is creativity so much your thing that it has to be central to your job? Or would you describe your creativity as intermittent? Getting the balance right is vital. You love melodrama: is chucking in your job as a youth worker and retraining to be an actor really what you want to do? If so, pursue it. But if you just need *some* aspect of melodrama in your life, try your local drama group first. Experiment with the balance.

✱ DREAM JOBBER

Laurie

Age: 63

Was: Businessman, Australia

Now: Science teacher, Sydney

Key to success: Recognizing when work was no longer fun

Passions: People, family

Here's a story about someone who had a rewarding career in business, but started to reassess his role and contribution in life.

Laurie is Australian and lives in Sydney. A childhood interest in physics led him to take a science degree before becoming a research officer in a huge industrial laboratory in one of Australia's largest glass-manufacturing companies. There he worked on problems related to the properties of glass and the thermal energy of glass furnaces. He really enjoyed this work. Like many people of his generation, he stayed with this company, very happily, long term. He travelled the world, got promoted and was able to go on researching the subject he was good at.

Then, at the age of 46, with five young children, Laurie left the company he had joined over twenty years earlier, and trained to become a teacher.

Five children! That's quite a financial commitment. Yet he ditched a very well-paid job, changed direction entirely, began again at the bottom, and even opted for a year without a salary at all.

How on earth did he manage to make that move? And what was it that made the move the right move?

To understand Laurie's decision, and its wisdom, you have to understand how Laurie operates, the kind of man he is, his values, his strengths and his weaknesses.

Laurie thoroughly enjoyed working for the company, he was competent and he felt recognized. Different jobs came his way. He didn't have to struggle for promotion. He was given a succession of interesting, rewarding and varied positions in different cities.

> After three and a bit years at the company, I was plucked out of the crowd and sent to the London office as a technical officer. In that job I was given the role of investigating various things in Europe. If there was something happening I was asked to go and have a look at it and report back to Australia, and as you might imagine it was a fabulous job and it entailed me travelling quite often to Holland, France, Spain and Germany and all around England and Wales. I enjoyed that immensely, but after two years I was brought back from there and given the job as the works chemist in the bottle factory in Melbourne. I did that for several years, then was moved to Sydney to do the same thing in a larger factory.

Whenever he expressed an interest in a new field, his bosses listened and gave him a new position with the opportunity to acquire new skills. In Laurie's story there is a constant sense of reward and development within a successful and well-managed company.

Sounds ideal, doesn't it? At this stage, Laurie had absolutely no reason to leave. His working environment was friendly, supportive and satisfying. By his own admission, Laurie says he's not particularly ambitious, but he had nevertheless reached the level of being, as he puts it, "quite a responsible person".

> I had been there for more than twenty years. I was quite well known. I felt comfortable within this environment. It was a company I well understood. It had policies, three-year plans, five-year plans. It had boards of directors, many of whom I knew – including the various chief executives.

As he explains, there may have been 25,000 employees, but it was like "being in a family".

But the bubble burst when the company experienced a series of takeovers. The working landscape began to change, the ethos changed with it and the management style became more cut-throat.

> It shattered the comfort of the company to suddenly be operated by managers whose style was aggressive, who threw out the five-year plans, who threw out the policies, because they found them too restrictive. Their philosophy was simply to maximize profits. Do it immediately, do it today, and if we have to change things in order to maximize profits tomorrow – then so be it.

Laurie's responsibilities as a manager began to change too. He returned to be head of the research laboratory he had started in, but now he had to cut its size down. In fact, he had to make a lot of people redundant. This way of working was alien to Laurie. Indeed, everything that he had valued about his working environment now began to slip away. He used to feel comfortable, now he felt increasingly uncomfortable.

He began to ask himself whether he really wanted to continue dedicating his life to making the perfect bottle.

> I started to realise, I guess with some considerable shock, that just because I had worked there for a long time my position wasn't necessarily valued. I found myself involved with retrenching staff, considering who might move, etc. The big change hit when it became obvious that the big research laboratory I was heading up was going to move from Sydney to Melbourne. It was assumed that I would go, I guess because I had worked in Melbourne once before. But I did say to my boss at the time, "Well, you know, if you were thinking of retrenching me then maybe I wouldn't mind so much." And he said, "No, certainly not." But several weeks later he said, "Now about what you said the other day, how do you feel about that?" So I was put in the position then of actually choosing whether I wanted to move to Melbourne or be retrenched. Our eldest was just leaving school and the youngest was less than twelve months old. We were pretty much locked into Sydney.

So Laurie, took a huge decision and opted for redundancy.

Redundancy, whether forced or voluntary, is an enormous change. "It was a huge risk," says Laurie, "I didn't know where it was going." But by the time he had made the decision to quit Laurie had done a number of things that made the transition feel less risky. By taking into consideration some straightforward, and rather obvious, key factors, something huge and daunting became small, manageable and ultimately realistic.

- Factor 1 was his ability to think positive. He sensed he could use this opportunity to make a constructive change in his life. "The realization came that there was something better to be doing."

- Factor 2 was his ability to analyse, reflect on and respond to his experience and behaviour. At some unconscious level, perhaps, he had been thinking and preparing for this move, because he now realized that he already had an idea of what he might choose for a new career.

  It wasn't a plan I had for a long time, it just became something that I grew into. I had over the previous two years or so had a little bit of experience in coaching a friend of mine in chemistry and in assisting other people and I felt I could kind of get the message across. It seemed to be that when I coached someone it was fairly well received. So I thought I might have the ability to be a teacher.

So, before he left his job, Laurie had an inkling of what he might do by looking at what he'd done in the past. He had also acquired recent experience that made him feel confident that he had some of the necessary skills for his new profession.

- Factor 3 was the moral element in Laurie's make-up. He felt teaching would be a good thing to do. Not just good for him, but good in an absolute sense.

  The really big thing that drove me towards it was that I wanted to be involved with people, and I wanted to be doing something *for* people. I had this perhaps quixotic view that being a teacher might help me to mould young minds and also, with my experience in industrial life, that I might be able to advise them on their career options. I had good intentions.

- Factor 4 was his preparation. He researched the field. He discovered that the New South Wales government was recruiting to train teachers. He made enquiries and established that he was eligible for a grant to retrain.

- Factor 5 was the redundancy money, which was enough to provide security for his family for twelve months, after which he would have to find a job if teaching didn't work out. He planned to use some of the money to pay off the mortgage so at least his family had the security of a home. Even so, was Laurie apprehensive about such an enormous change at this stage in his life?

Certainly. I had five children, one of whom was very young. I was forgoing a pretty substantial salary and moving into teaching, which was hardly financially lucrative.

● There was also Factor 6, the vital (for him) support of his family.

My wife Marie was very supportive of what I was doing and was quite keen for me to get out of the company that had swallowed my life for so long. She was supportive of my ideals.

With those factors in place, Laurie was able to feel more confident about the move. It felt right. "I left the company and embarked on my new career, my second life."

What Laurie wanted from work was intellectual stimulation and variety within a secure environment where he could interact with and find support from others. He wasn't driven by personal ambition, and was reactive more than he was proactive. But he liked a level of responsibility and over time proved his value to the business in which he worked and to which he felt he belonged.

The four things that enabled him to have the confidence to make a career change were:

1   Changes in his work environment that "shattered the comfort".

2   His desire to do valuable work.

3   A substantial pay-off, which provided some security for his family.

4   The support of his family.

He made an enormous change, but he coped with it because he loved having the opportunity to study again, to re-engage with intellectual material. He also enjoyed being with young people and the companionship of working with fellow students.

> To go back to university at a mature age and to actually have the time to sit in the library to research things and grapple with science subjects was fantastic! I wasn't quite the oldest student – there was one older! But most of them were in their mid-twenties. But we were a good group and I enjoyed it immensely.

He graduated and succeeded in getting a job as a science teacher in Sydney. But how did he find making the transition from being a businessman for 25 years to working as a newly qualified teacher? It wasn't easy. He found the job itself challenging and difficult.

> I found preparing lessons extremely hard work and I had great difficulties in crowd control and in the discipline side of things. Although there was good support from the teachers within the science department, I have to say after eighteen months I wondered why I was doing it!

Unfortunately, he didn't find the working environment congenial.

> While there were good teaching staff, there was no particular feeling among colleagues that we were all pulling together to do a particular job. There was no sense from the students that we were helping them and there was no particular support from the parents. It was a state school in a blue-collar area where most students were leaving at fifteen or sixteen to get apprenticeships. Not many went on to university.

While in business, Laurie had always worked in a supportive and rewarding environment. He didn't feel this school provided it. He started to have reservations about his new career.

> Did I have doubts? Yes. I hadn't been getting that much satisfaction from doing it. It was a really hard slog, and I worked harder than I seemed to remember working in my previous life! So yes, I guess I was doubting if I had made the right decision.

To achieve job satisfaction, Laurie knew he needed three things – support, a sense of teamwork and like-minded colleagues. Having taken a gamble and retrained, he had ended up in a job he didn't particularly enjoy.

So he took another chance. He knew two people at another school, a friend and a cousin, and they both suggested he apply for a job there. Once again, he didn't particularly take the initiative and go looking for change. The school he had landed up in didn't provide what he wanted, and it took other people to make him consider moving.

> So I wrote to this other school, a large Jesuit school in Sydney. I detailed my qualifications. I said "this is me" and "this is why you should have me". It seemed to work. I received a reply from the deputy headmaster, who asked me to come in and talk to him. Then subsequently, a couple of weeks later, I was asked to come and meet the headmaster, which I did, and they seemed to be interested in me, but there was no job available at the time. So three or four months later they contacted me and asked if I was still interested. But they said, "We can only guarantee you a job for nine months covering for long service leave and maternity leave – but we'd love to have you and we'll see what happens after that."

> So that was another major decision for me. Do I leave my secure job and join another school for what might be only a temporary job? It didn't take too long to figure out "yes, that's a good idea, that's what I want to do". With my wife's support I chose to leave the state school and take my chances by joining St Ignatius College.

In his search for something more fulfilling with a similar ethos to his own, Laurie took a risk. He could have been out of work in nine months. But at least, from the research he had done, the school sounded promising. How did this new job compare?

> Well, what a difference. St Ignatius College had a staff who were most welcoming and friendly and who met and chatted with each other every day in the common room and at morning tea and at lunch, and there was a tremendous feeling of collegiality among the staff. We were all there doing the same job – namely to do the best we could for the boys of the college. It was commonplace for science teachers to talk to art teachers, to talk to history teachers, etc. – to share experiences, to share plans and best teaching methods for pupils. There was a great opportunity for sharing thoughts about what was best for the boys. This feeling that all the staff were working together to ensure the best outcome was tremendously refreshing. The boys themselves wanted to be at the school, a little bit reluctantly, but not too much. They recognized that they were there to learn. And the parents were most supportive and interested in how their sons were getting on. Mind you, the fees they were being charged, that's probably not surprising! I relished the change: it was such a difference to be working in a Christian environment, to be with people who wanted to be there, to be sharing this great venture of educating boys. So this was finally what I had thought teaching was going to be like. So I revelled in it. I still had to work hard. It was a demanding school in terms of the subjects, sport commitments and other school duties, including pastoral care.

The gamble of leaving his other job also paid off when, after nine months, the school was able to offer Laurie a full-time job. To date, Laurie is still there and loving it!

Laurie found like-minded teachers and students and that was the key to him enjoying his job as a teacher. As a businessman, he had always had supportive, positive working environments. When that changed, he left. Working in a school that didn't share the same hopes and values he had about the profession made him question his suitability for the job. But transferring to a new school, which mirrored his own hopes for the profession, enabled him to settle in and enjoy it. Right job, wrong environment. Laurie went on to pursue particular areas of work which he found really fulfilling. This let him get to know the boys and their families and care for their progression and well-being.

A feature of Laurie's story is his Christian faith. At the most difficult times he put his faith in God. You may or may not be religious, but you need to get confidence and trust from somewhere – perhaps your family or friends, or your life coach, or simply your gut instinct and your accumulated experience of life. It will help you put trust in your future and take away some of the fear.

LAURIE'S ADVICE

1   I'm fortunate that I had the opportunity to have two different careers. The first career was the more highly paid and it gave me the opportunity to raise a family and to buy a house and become settled. I don't know how we would have coped if I'd been a teacher all my life.

2   But to change one's job in middle age and to take on another – well, I believe I've been very blessed with that opportunity. Would I do it again? Yes, I think I would! It's been a great journey and I didn't know that it was going to be like this when I first left school or university. There was certainly no plan, it just happened.

3   I believe if you take the opportunity when it comes and if you enter into a second career with an open mind and a desire to do well at it, ride with the punches and take it as it comes, then I think happiness comes from that.

Laurie's life is dominated by work, but also by family. He finds both hugely rewarding. As a contrast, I want to introduce Jason, who had the opportunity to work in the family business, but needed to get out and find his own way. He headed off on his motorbike to do precisely that.

✳ DREAM JOBBER

Jason

Age: 38

Was: Builder, UK

Now: Photographer, India

Key to success: Found a way of life first

Passions: Music, photography, motorbikes

Jason is a freelance photographer. He is British, but he lives in India. To understand why, one needs to understand him and, above all, his values. Of course, the real key to Jason's choice of job and lifestyle is that *he*, Jason, has come to understand himself and, above all, his values.

So what sort of a person is he? He's lean, muscular, intense, passionate. He loves cooking, sensory experience and not knowing what's next.

> I've always been very strong in myself, confident, adventurous and self-sufficient. The thought of settling down has always scared me, the thought of having to limit where I go and how long I can go for. Maybe it's a bit of a selfish way to exist but it's a life that makes me feel stronger. I've always lived in a fairly self-contained world, but not everyone does. Maybe I've just been lucky, maybe I will never marry, maybe I will never have much money and maybe I will die

young, but I am willing to forfeit all the above in exchange for my experiences and happiness.

Jason's very independent minded, and he needs to feel untrammelled and free.

I left school with O levels in woodwork and art. To begin with I worked for my father, and trained and worked in carpentry and welding. Later I went into landscape gardening with various stints at university, working in restaurants and selling things in various markets around London. From the age of seventeen, when I went out and bought a Triumph Bonneville to tour around Europe, it's been a bit of a problem staying in one place – too much to see and too little time to see it all.

But eventually, following a stint at university studying business, and four years into a relationship, he and his girlfriend needed a mortgage, so he ended up settling down and selling houses.

How I hated that job. Life went into slow motion and every day was a struggle. My letter of resignation was sitting there in my desk drawer from day one. I travelled to work by motorbike dressed in jeans, bought myself an old suit from the charity shop and took the interesting clients out in the manager's car for long drives around the area. The day I succeeded in getting a mortgage I walked out the door. Never again. But it was an important part of the process, to know the direction you really don't want to go in.

He split up with his girlfriend and bought a ticket to India. He disappeared off into the mountains on his own, went trekking and exploring. It was a period of time out and reflection.

I ended up floating in the warm waters of the Indian Ocean facing the palm groves and mountains and wondered how you could ever have a job that would enable you to spend most of your time in places as beautiful and peaceful. It was five years and a variety of

Krishnamurti's books before I realized how to achieve this. To me, life and work are one and the same. My way of life came first, then the necessity to make money came later. It takes time to establish yourself in your chosen field, but in the end it's the most amazing feeling.

The trip to India proved a life-changing experience.

It exposed me to issues that had a profound effect on me. I never really realized that things could be that bad. It was a big wake-up call. I went from what I felt to be a sterile, Western, middle-class environment to the madness of the East and its constant stimulation of the senses – some good, some bad, but always making you engage with your environment. Once I'd experienced this, I wanted to have more.

Without any future plans at this stage, he returned to the UK to work and earn money. He stayed for four years. He joined a company doing landscape gardening. It was physical, it was outdoors and it gave him the flexibility to travel in the winter. He was still working out where he really wanted to be and what he wanted to do. He knew he would be leaving soon. He was just waiting for the right moment.

And while he enjoyed the practical work to start with, he found the owners didn't share his values. He felt they had no commitment to quality, to craftsmanship. They were out to cut corners and compromise standards. It led increasingly to jobs he didn't enjoy.

Seventy per cent of the time was spent working in horrid modern housing developments digging up builders' rubble while people nit-picked about the colour of the grass or complained that one of the bricks was a slightly different shade. Lots of the work became frustrating, backbreaking, with little creative input. Running my own company would have been easy, but it would have meant employing people and eventually removing myself from doing the one thing I really enjoyed. I wanted to spend more time on a project, finish the job properly. Less and less cement went in the mix and the lies increased stress levels. It ended up representing everything I didn't want to be a part of.

Unable to stand it any longer, he quit and turned to his father's carpentry business. His father set about training him to take it over. Jason still loves the demands of a highly skilled profession like carpentry. Unfortunately he experienced the same obsessive money-making mentality he'd witnessed in the landscape garden industry. He simply didn't share his father's values. The promise of two cars and retirement by 40 rang hollow for him. "What do you do after that when you have the cars and you've paid off the mortgage?"

Sensing that his future was being mapped out for him, Jason knew he needed liberty and to be self-sufficient. It was a significant time and, following a family argument, he turned his back on his family's plans for him. He went off in search of himself and the right lifestyle.

When he left the family business he rode his motorbike down to Bordeaux and stayed with friends who'd bought a place, and he helped with its renovation. Then he went to Switzerland and worked in a factory. This ride represented "total freedom".

> I was leaving the family and the business behind. I was isolated and I realised I couldn't go back. I set about finding my own way.

And finding his own way eventually led him to photography, which he feels "had always been there". Jason describes himself as a visual person, and rather than write about some of the amazing things he witnessed he began to photograph them. Following some reiki treatments ("which I never really believed in at the time"), "There seemed to be a fundamental shift in my outlook and confidence; I made the decision to change, and all of a sudden things became more clear, who I was and where I should be going."

With encouragement from a friend he decided to pursue an emerging dream. "By this time I had nothing to lose." He returned to India with his camera in the hope he could create some sort of livelihood.

> I kept finding myself in the most amazing situations with the most amazing people, stories that people would never believe. So I started to take photographs. It was a very natural thing to do, just continue doing what I did but every now and then pick up the camera.
>
> I immersed myself in the environment and learnt to be a photographer. I hung around trying to understand photography. I spent time with heroin addicts, street families, drug dealers. It opened my mind up and made me question, mix with different people and witness the disparities in society. I got beaten up by the police, arrested and interrogated for twelve hours. I constantly try to push myself. It's like diving into the deep end. Your radar comes out and you work things out by instinct. You don't experience life if you're too methodical. So I let things happen.

After that he did some work for the British Council, and commissions slowly began to come in. He would go back to the UK, and try to get work commissioned from newspapers to enable him to go off for another six months. But trying to exist in both countries became too difficult and eventually he stopped coming back to England. He put the few things he had into cardboard boxes in various friends' attics and moved into a flat in Delhi.

> Committing to India, I learnt that I could still get work with international organizations. This year I've had one job for five days and that's given me enough to fund my work all year. I've got a feature coming up in a national newspaper. It's about the Dongria Kondh tribe in a remote area of Orissa, India, which I've been working on for about a year. I want to show people the human cost of industrialization in remote areas by using the images I take in

different ways. I target publications and work closely with relevant organizations.

But he realized that, to do the subjects justice, he had to spend time with them, otherwise it became a voyeuristic pursuit. He wanted to make a real difference.

> At first I romanticized the whole concept of being a roaming photographer coming to developing countries to aid the helpless. Now I realize that for most photographers, with their over-inflated egos, it's more about them, their next book, their next exhibition. I could never do it. I'm not saying that I don't make money, I do (I have to), but most of what I earn is ploughed back into the project I work on, or it's used to purchase new equipment so that I can move forward in my work.

So what is it like, this lifestyle that Jason has spent so long tracking down and setting up?

> One day you are flying business class and staying in five-star hotels, then the next job you are in the middle of a forest, sick, cold and hungry, and it's pouring with rain. I feel more alive and more at home in the second one. I feel more connected to what I'm doing, although I would find it difficult to permanently survive in that environment. It's a tough existence, but really makes you appreciate the simple pleasures of life.

> I'm constantly looking for new ways to develop my work and find new ways to communicate the issues I work on. This takes time to do it any justice. I worked on a project looking at destigmatization of Indian truck drivers linked to HIV/AIDS. I spent three months travelling around the country in trucks, sleeping on the side of the road, cooking meals in the cab, washing in rivers. Everyone told me that ten days was all that I needed, but I felt it was impossible to understand their issues without living with them. The project ended with a series of exhibitions and a CD-ROM of the work. It was because

I funded myself, built up such a body of work and understood their environment that people trusted and believed in me on future projects. It may have been two years of self-funded work, but it's now starting to pay off. If you don't have too many expectations, things will start to form and fall into place.

What about the down days?

Lots of self-doubt, all the time, but that's what keeps you on your toes – you try so much harder because you are convinced the work is never good enough. I spend months on a project trying to get funding, banging my head against the wall, ending up alone in hotel rooms crying and wondering where to go next or frustrated about the injustices of the world. But it's all part of the process and you only come out stronger at the end of it. Sometimes, I really understand why people take up careers that only stimulate wealth growth and not personal development! It's difficult to face everything the world has to throw at you, I can only take so much, then have to hide for a few days. India is perfect for me. Some have too much, but most have nothing and never will. It's difficult having to move between the two, you don't feel that you belong to either, and you don't want to. I would not have done anything differently. It's all been very good so far. The pain is just as important as the pleasure!

Any regrets?

I'm happy, I have my moments as we all do, and finally I've started to make some money. I tend to gauge my success on the success of my work and the impact it has. The money is fairly low on the list, although it is very much a necessity to continue in what I am doing. I've been able to make a living because I've stuck with it, understood my environment and become passionate about the issues I work with. That comes through in your work, and people respond to it.

Jason could easily have settled for a comfortable life within his family's successful furniture business, earning good money and having a wealthy and secure life. But Jason's values demanded much more than that. Even if it means that he has to endure discomfort, danger or poverty, his values (justice, freedom and hedonism) drove him to seek an unconventional life and career path. Doing what he feels is some good in the world is his true vocation. To do it he needed a lifestyle that was right *for him*. That meant he had to feel free. He ensures that he commits to nothing that will limit that feeling of freedom. So rather than have a permanent home with a mortgage and regular bills to pay, he stays at friends' houses, or he moves between locations – a beach hut in Goa, a flat in Delhi.

And he found a profession – photography – that fitted such a lifestyle and allowed him to express his moral and political passion. He made sure he became a skilled photographer, and he found a niche that allowed him to earn a living while exposing the injustices that make him so passionate.

He has no idea what the future holds. His girlfriend has just returned to America to study policy and development.

> This caused me to reflect on a variety of issues and question certain elements of my life, particularly the insecurity I have, which relates to finding it difficult to sustain any long-term relationship – and whether I ever will. I do want it very much. At the moment, I know that if I go and visit my girlfriend, which I really want to do, it takes me away from my work. I need to be immersed in it. I'm about to go to Orissa. It's a three-day journey by train. I face mosquitoes, scorpions, snakes. It's like jumping into a cold swimming pool. There's that apprehension before you do it, but once you do it's OK. But who wouldn't want to do it? It's exciting. It's unique and I feel privileged to experience it. It's been eight years now, and it's been a long and hard journey, but I have never felt I've made a mistake and never looked back to where I could have been.

JASON'S ADVICE

1 I think making change is very much to do with the dictates of society, family pressures and people being able to understand your own limitations. I've met so many people who will never be what they dream of being. I think that many people leave it too late, then make an extreme decision based more on desperation than anything else.

2 It's a very personal thing, but self-belief is essential – that, and perhaps a very understanding family.

3 I also think people feel they need more than they really do. It's about giving up all those little comfortable things in life, at least for a while.

4 It's a difficult transition to make to give up so much for the unknown, but it really is worth it if you can make that first step.

 There's always a little prick ready to burst your bubble.

COUNTDOWN TO YOUR DREAM JOB
Carole Ann's career coaching boot camp

When we don't live in our values, conflict can arise. You feel uncomfortable, as if you don't fit in and are working against your natural instincts and the world around you. Both Laurie and Jason felt this psychic "friction", despite having two completely differing life stories.

At the beginning of his career Laurie loved what he was doing, enjoyed the work, and the challenges and travelling that came with it. He was successful and promotion came easy.

It wasn't Laurie but the job which changed, and soon he found himself undertaking tasks such as making people redundant which didn't sit well with him or his values. This was his spur to move on.

Jason too could have easily settled for a comfortable life within his family's successful furniture business, earning good money and having a wealthy and secure life. But Jason's values demanded more, propelling him to seek an unconventional life and career path.

When do you feel like you're pushing against something? When are you at your best?

THE BIG QUESTIONS

Many years ago the writers, artists and philosophers of the Left Bank of Paris called it "existentialist angst", which simply means the agony of asking why we are here. It may be a big question with an even bigger answer, but for coaches it's a good starting point in helping people get real about what they want to do with their lives. It may be scary, but it's thrilling fun too. Just as life changes should be.

So take your notebook and ask yourself:

1 Why am I here?

Now think – is it to have fun, make a difference, be remembered, help others, to entertain, teach, guide, harmonize, party or be the best?

Write down anything – it's your life, after all – that comes into your head. What might be your life purpose? Don't worry if it sounds odd, ludicrous or unobtainable – it's your vision, so don't judge it.

2 What is it I want to do with the time I have left?

So, looking at the first question, are some thoughts coming through? Would you like to teach, make a difference in other people's lives, be helpful, creative? Maybe the desire to explore, design or inspire could be signposts directing you to explore more fully. Can you imagine what it would be like to do those things and get paid for them? You can, and other people do.

3   What is required of me?

This is a call to action. What do you need to do to start fulfilling your life's purpose? What would you be prepared to commit to, let go of or invest in? The rewards for living your life as you were destined to are vast, infinite even. Will you give yourself permission to reach for them?

Write down your answers, and go back and reread them, often.

CHAPTER **5**

ACTION IS ALL

"When I recovered [from cancer], I realized that life is too short not to do something you really want to do … I'm not qualified to do what I do. I'm not really qualified to do anything. I keep thinking I'll be sitting round the table having dinner and someone will come up to me and tap me on the back and say 'we've found you out'. But it does seem to be working so far. "

Cath Kidston (interior designer, UK)[1]

Are you clear about what you *don't* want to do, but not clear about what you *do* want to do?

In the past I used to draw up lists, I compiled scrapbooks, lists of dream jobs I was unqualified for, all in a desperate attempt to find something that would tell me what I should do with my life. I stared long and hard and nothing came. I went back to the same old, same old. I was totally trapped by the "not knowing".

And it's the same with so many of my interviewees. People in desperate need of change were nevertheless in a state of paralysis about their situation. They had no idea how to move forward, much less where to move to. In some cases there was no time to even plan change, and in others there was so much space that not coming into contact with anyone or anything new meant total stasis prevailed.

Finding your purpose is essential. But don't panic if you haven't been struck by a career-changing bolt of lightning.

Having some awareness of your values and what you enjoy is all you require at this stage, although for some people even this will not be entirely clear. If that resonates, you just need to be open to finding out as you enter the next phase.

Support from other people is always useful, so ask for it. People don't know you need assistance, advice and guidance unless you voice that need. And people like being asked. One day, you will be able to help someone else.

ACTION IS ALL

Now is not the time for reflection. Now is the time for DOING. It's all about making a first move, being hands-on, trying things out.

Do one thing today for yourself. One phone call, or one email to request a cup of coffee with someone who can give you advice or information. Find an article about a job or a person that sounds interesting to you. Tomorrow do the same. Take this opportunity to explore a range of future possibilities. All those things you "might like" – make this your chance to find out. Explore three areas you think you might want to work in. Then shortlist two more!

People don't know you are keen and available unless you tell them, and employers might just be looking for someone like you. It's worth taking a chance. What's the worst that can happen?

✳ DREAM JOBBER

Renaud

Age: 28

Was: Hospital worker, France

Now: Assistant textile designer, UK

Key to success: Dared to take a chance

Passions: Music, fashion, food

Born and brought up in France, Renaud took a chance when he noticed pots and paintbrushes through the window of a design studio while he was house-hunting in South London. He was trying to embark on a new life and had spent the day looking at dodgy flats. Up to this point, he had been working in a hospital in France. His chosen career had been on hold after he failed to get his diploma at a highly competitive art college in Brussels. A year working in his home town with elderly patients had helped him put life into perspective, and he felt it was time to resume his dream of a career in fashion. So here he was, one dismal evening in London, trying to find accommodation and embark on a new life. He took a deep breath and plucked up the courage to stick his head round the door of an inviting-looking studio to ask for a job.

> I was waiting for the last viewing of a flat to be perfect. It was the worst! It was 6 p.m., dark and cold in December. I left this horrible flat, walking in the streets feeling lost and lonely, when I saw this multicoloured shop window full of beautiful paintings, designs, fabrics. It was as inviting as a patisserie where you pop in to get something delicious! My only concern was that I didn't want to purchase a dozen gorgeous macaroons but to get a job! "Let's think about it and walk a bit," I said to myself. "I should walk in confidently and ask for a job. But maybe it's not a studio? My English is much too bad. I don't have my CV or my portfolio ..." However, I told myself I could still try!

So Renaud went in. He spoke to Sarah, one of the textile designers at work in the front of the shop. She was incredibly approachable, and told him that she co-owned the studio with her sister, Susan, and that, by sheer coincidence, they were currently looking for someone to employ! She gave him her business card and asked him to call her in January when he was back from France and could bring in his portfolio.

> I was really shy and worried about my spoken English. At the same time a little voice in my head told me not to worry about things, but to do it now. If I reflected too much it would be too late, I would miss precious opportunities. "If I just ask, they might say no, but also they may say yes!" The more you take decisions and take opportunities, the more you feel confident to find your own way ... So I did it. I try as

much as I can to be strong and never stay in my comfort zone. To feel alive, I have to constantly challenge my thoughts and behaviour …

Renaud remained committed. He sent them some examples of his work, but they advised him to get more experience of colour work. He returned to France and did just that. He sent them new examples of his designs, applied for a grant and was soon able to inform the sisters that if they accepted him he could handle all the necessary paperwork. All they had to do was agree. By organizing his own work experience, Renaud had quickly landed a new life in London, and it soon led to his being offered a paid position as an assistant textile designer in their studio.

RENAUD'S ADVICE

1 Take small steps, be persistent, be patient. Trying only once won't necessarily bring about change. You need to keep at it.

2 Although failing at the art college in Brussels left me distraught at the time and depressed for a year, now I'm glad I didn't get it. In hindsight, I now understand that I wasn't good enough and I was wrong about what I thought about fashion. Bad experiences can be as illuminating and as valuable as good ones. In my case it led to an extremely rewarding year out working with people where it really mattered.

3 Unless you get out there and tell them, people don't know you're looking. Only through experimenting, researching and engaging with the world will you unearth your true vocation.

 Nothing comes of nothing. There are no wrong moves. If you're stuck in a rut, the only wrong move at this stage is no move at all.

✱ DREAM JOBBER

Deborah

Age: 46

Was: Actress, UK

Now: Director of own company, UK

Key to success: "I aim to be the best at what I do"

Passion: Helping people feel better about themselves

Deborah is director of her own company, Heaven Skincare Products, and a beauty therapist. But, if it helps, at the start of her career Deborah had no idea what to do. It was through "doing" and trying things out that she found her vocation in life. Now her pioneering beauty treatments have gone international, she has her own factory, and her organic products attract celebrity clients.

For a woman who is so obviously in the right job, it's interesting to discover that she came to it by accident. As a teenager Deborah experimented with various potential careers, including modelling and drama, but nothing felt like the right vocation. One of her friends was a hairdresser and suggested she try beauty therapy. Deborah thought she might as well sort out her acne problem while she worked out what she wanted to do with her life. She describes the sensation she experienced the moment she began to practise treatments on other students, however, as "coming home". By chance, and by doing, she had found something that appealed to her, excited her and tapped into her need to help other people.

> Healing my skin made me feel better about how I looked. I wanted to help other people feel good about themselves too. The moment I tried

it out, I realized that beauty therapy enabled me to do this – I could connect with people and heal them.

Deborah had been shopping around looking for a career, but nothing had appealed. Rather than sit and wait for divine intervention, she opted to "do" during one of many "don't know" phases, and she eventually found something that completely switched her on. Stumbling across beauty therapy has led to the creation of a very valuable business. Deborah created the Heaven skincare range, which has featured in *Vogue* and *Harpers & Queen*. Kylie and Dannii Minogue are fans, and entrepreneurs Theo Paphitis and Richard Branson have offered investment and, in one case, a job – which she declined. A high-street chain wanted to make the products in their factories, but such is her integrity and commitment to making truly pure products, Deborah opted to remain independent. She went on to take a huge financial risk by buying her own factory, where she can control and ensure the production of skin treatments that are genuinely organic and preservative free. Her aim is to spread healing through skin – not sell out and jeopardize the quality of the product.

FINDING THE "SOMETHING"

The "something" will feel good, positive and motivating. There might be a connection with what you did as a child, and once you find the something, it may feel blindingly obvious, as it did for Deborah.

> In hindsight, I now remember I mixed flower potions as a child and kept them under the bed – which probably wasn't unusual for a six-year-old. However, slightly more unusually, I also added a touch of vodka to keep the flowers preserved! I was experimenting with concoctions even then. Now I'm here I can see my business makes sense, but I didn't know until I was actually *doing* it.

As Steve Jobs says, you can only "join the dots" up in hindsight. But you need to trust that every step you take will join up eventually.

Finance was another "dot" from Deborah's childhood which played an important role in her future. As a child she would set herself financial challenges to fund the things she wanted. Using every tactic she could think of to economize, fourteen-year-old Deborah would walk home to avoid the bus fare and save her lunch money. After saving enough for a leather jacket (£18.95 back then), she then decided to save £250 for a horse.

> It took two years but I did it! But once I got the horse I needed to get a job to keep it. So I got a job as a waitress working nights. I then pushed to make the sandwiches. Without being told, I would improvise and make garnishes to perfect the presentation. I was ticked off for wasting tomatoes, but for me the presentation is important. Even from such an early age, I was someone who wanted to be the best at what I do.

This was an approach she also applied when she started her beauty training course. Using her initiative rather than following the rules, Deborah continued to improvise and explore.

> In the early days of the course, a facial cream reacted with my skin. Instinctively I began to play around with the mixture and I added a balm used in leg waxing to create something soothing rather than abrasive. Everyone else was doing what they were told to do – but I just got on and experimented.

As we have seen, Deborah had been working, saving up and balancing her own finances from an early age. So she found the basic business skills and "cheque writing" session on the course unenlightening. As she stared out of the window during one class, she had a clear vision about her future, and she pictured herself running her own mobile business and salons, and then franchising them out. By imagining her future, she could literally see where she was going. From this moment, Deborah had a clear plan of action.

"You need to work out where you're going," she says adamantly. "If you don't, you'll never get there. It's like going to London without knowing where you're aiming for. How will you ever reach your destination?"

First, to put her plan into action Deborah needed experience. She astutely noted that the other students would be looking for a job at the end of the course in May, so she pre-empted the stampede, and started looking at Christmas. She gave herself the best chance possible of getting into her chosen, competitive field. And, whatever happened, at least she would have a job. "I succeeded in my search for a job and was hired at a local salon. And while I was really quite good, I was very shy," she admits. "It was very valuable because they made me talk to the customers, and it gave me tactics to deal with my shyness."

So, shyness is no barrier to success. Talking to Deborah now, she doesn't seem at all shy. She is full of energy, positivity, determination. But she does admit that shyness remains a battle for her, and she attends her PR events only when forced to. While she finds networking and talking about herself excruciating, however, talking about, presenting and selling her products is second nature. Inhibitions often fall away when talking about your passions.

BUILDING THE BUSINESS

From the outset of her career, Deborah looked for ways to expand the business, accumulating her skills and experience. By investing in a box of nail extensions, for example, she learnt to do nails. This brought in money to buy other things. After three years Deborah moved to a salon in Wolverhampton. She got married, left and, following the master plan, set up her mobile business.

It took several attempts to contact Deborah, as she's a very busy person. I talked to her over the phone while she was cooking the dinner (the only "free time" she had). She broke off periodically to talk to her children.

On the surface, the story she told me seemed very easy and straightforward. But in fact it involved plenty of hurdles. For example, she split up from her first husband, but, continuing to "do" rather than sit back or give up, in that very same week she opened her first shop. She has a blindingly positive approach to her business. "I'd set up in a health club but I had too many clients. I needed new premises and a base to work from."

Deborah's the type of person who doesn't understand the word "no". As the business grew, she built up a team of beauticians to cope with demand. When that was up and running she opened another shop. The business continued to mushroom. Today she is securing contracts with high-street retailers to stock her products. Her pioneering LIA skincare treatment is now international. Publicity and celebrity clients are a part of everyday life.

> I love my work so much that being with the customers for me is relaxation. I care about my staff and clients and I love working. So much so, I don't like or take holidays. I'm always thinking about work. If I go for a coffee I'll work out the number of covers and the amount of profit that could be made in a café. It's automatic and not work – it's just how my mind operates.

She admits to being competitive. She describes herself as a leader. But she sees herself as a collective leader. "I want my family and a team to be swept along with me. I need lots of people around and to pull them along. It's in you to do it." She is alone in that she is the sole director; it means she is lonely sometimes, but she doesn't want to share that role because she can't stand people telling her what to do. That has been the case from birth!

Deborah demonstrates the classic traits of an entrepreneur – constantly on the lookout for new business ideas and dreaming up new formulas. But I'd just like to point out that Deborah says *she loves her work so much it's relaxation.* Who's ever heard of a job being *relaxing*! Mini-breaks are not required. Being at work for Deborah is a holiday.

As I hear her talk about the new shops, the new factories, the offers of new income streams, the celebrity clients and the new treatments, I want to know how she finds the nerve to do it. Is there never a fear of failing, losing money, not being able to pay staff? Are there really no sleepless nights?

> Personally, I find it's harder to walk away from something that is difficult than to try it and fail. You'll spend the rest of your life regretting and wondering "what if". If you just try something and it fails, it's over quickly and you can move on to the next thing. But there have been times when money's been scarce and I needed more orders to pay wages. Again I had to keep positive and I hoped and wished for more orders, and eventually, they came.

Obviously, wishful thinking doesn't always bring in new orders! But being able to trust that orders/work/clients will come is an important part of the process. If you are doing something you believe in and are aiming to be the best at what you do, selling pure, quality products for which you believe there is a market, you simply need to make a decision about continuing or not. Is it likely more orders will come in? Or is it not worth risking your staff and house to keep the business going? In Deborah's case she held her nerve, hoped for the best for her quality products and pioneering treatments – and the orders came in. Learning to trust takes away anxiety. And it helps you to move on rather than get bogged down in "Should I? Shouldn't I?"

As well as coping with the fear of not attracting enough custom, Deborah has had to combat thieves. Her products are so good that a rival manufacturer stole her formulas and copied them.

> I was convinced I was ruined. After agonizing for four days, I came up with the solution. I decided to remake the products – *but take advantage of the situation by improving the products at the same time.* I went on to create a far superior best-seller. If the formulas hadn't been stolen, I wouldn't have made the new products. I try and think there are no setbacks in life, just ways of teaching me things.

From an early age, Deborah proved she is someone who can handle difficulties. Another snapshot from her childhood reveals a person who likes to put herself to the test (to say the least!). "I would make myself jump off the garage roof to see if I had the nerve to do it. I remember the thrill when I succeeded." Deborah needs challenges, adrenalin and excitement, and won't be happy in the security and dullness of the comfort zone.

Deborah has created a working life that is so enjoyable it feels like an indulgence. Money is still scarce sometimes, but her business is now valuable. "And as long as I've got my hands," she says, "I know I can pay the bills." She found a vocation she truly enjoys by trying things out. She rejected what didn't excite her and kept on looking until she found something that really switched her on. She was open to new experiences and noticed when it felt right. "Confronting the fear of the unknown," she advises, "is better than living with a decision that you don't agree with."

DEBORAH'S ADVICE

1 Think about what it is you want and write a list.

2 Keep on *doing* until you find "the thing" that feels like "coming home". Keep your motivations at the heart of the job. I wanted to sell pure, organic products to help people feel better about themselves – not to sell out and make money with an inferior product.

3 Don't get bogged down with the "what if?" in life, just get on with it, the trying, failing and succeeding.

4 Attempting to change career may well feel like chucking yourself off the garage roof – scary and somewhat foolish. But if you are feeling frightened then this is good and it is natural. It's HUGE. You are beginning to see that there may be some exciting things out there calling for your attention.

✱ DREAM JOBBER

Achilles

Age: 42

Was: Photocopying engineer, Australia

Now: Wine merchant, Australia

Key to success: Outgoing and friendly personality

Passions: Electronics/technology, wine, food, music

In spite of being a natural "doer", Achilles got stuck in his job and lost the confidence to try to move.

Achilles has been "doing" since he was born. Constantly fiddling with electronics as a child, he built his own FM radio station for his town. He and his friends would broadcast on station "UFO", operating at midnight after the TV station closed! A pretty extraordinary achievement for a fourteen-year-old. The "doing" continued when he got a job working for a company which enabled him to continue tinkering as he fixed photocopiers for a living. After eighteen years, though, he tired of mending and "doing" round the back of the fuser unit, and started exploring possible new futures. He is now an area manager for a wine distributor in Australia. At the same time, the science of winemaking appeals to him, and he hopes eventually to produce his own wine as a career.

I met Achilles at his home in Melbourne. He is a man of many talents, including cooking and music – it had been his boyhood fascination with electronics, music and audio which led him to want to become an audio and visual media engineer.

> I studied electronics at technical high school in Greece, but I was actually born in Australia, and came back and enrolled on a course at the Royal Melbourne Institute of Technology with government financial assistance. Within a year my parents also returned to Melbourne, and I had to look for work to support them financially. At the time there were not many employment opportunities for engineers in audio/visual media. So, when I came across a job as a photocopier engineer I jumped at the chance. I was twenty at the time and happy to be earning a good salary for doing something I was interested in and was good at. Plus at that age having a company car was a thrill and I also had access to camera supplies, which suited my photographic hobbies.

At the time, the prospect of this first job felt stable and rewarding. Visiting different companies provided some variety in the places and people Achilles met, but there were the obvious downsides too.

> I would say "hello" to the client and get straight on to diagnosing what the problem with the machine was. Usually I'd be on my hands and knees looking for some minute movable part that was the culprit. Always fixing people's problems meant that I would be the brunt of client frustrations and anger – everyone hates it when their photocopier is on the blink! The nature of this corporate environment meant that personnel constantly changed and so I never developed relationships with clients. I would rush in, get the job done as quickly as possible, and rush to the next problem. On the other hand, seeing so many different people was one thing that kept me interested. I never knew who I would meet next.

But Achilles was wary of the chemicals he was dealing with. The toner is a carcinogen that photocopier engineers come into contact with every day. This was always in the back of his mind. In addition, as he got older and continued to scrabble around on his knees every day, the physical demands of the job became harder. He became aware that it was unlikely he could carry on in such a job until retirement. Even so, by the end, the biggest problem for Achilles was the boredom.

So why did he stay for eighteen years? What stopped him from leaving?

> I was paying my family's mortgage and needed a steady income. Even so, I would have got out of the job earlier, but I didn't really think I was capable of doing anything else other than fixing machines. I didn't want to risk it. And it was too easy to stay. I was quite happy for a long time, focusing on all my other pursuits beyond work (community theatre, wedding DJ, singing in choirs, acting, sound engineer). And I had close friendships with the other staff, friendships which distracted me from the boredom of the job. I'd go to the market, cook up fish and meat for the staff, and we'd have fun "souvlaki Fridays" together.

Clearly, Achilles was a "doer", with rewarding extra-curricular activities. His outgoing personality ensured he engaged with his job and with his work colleagues. It was a people-oriented job which required interaction. But eventually he needed to move on. So what finally enabled Achilles to overcome his fears of "risking it all" and make a successful career change?

> It wasn't just the repetition of tasks and lack of challenge, I just have so many other interests that excite me that this job eventually made me feel I was wasting my life. I got to a point where I couldn't bear the boredom and wasted potential any longer. I began to feel trapped, which made me quite depressed. I got to the point where the pain of staying in this job was worse than the risk of leaving it for something new. It became obvious that using the job to support my out-of-work interests was no longer enough.

And one particular 'out-of-work' interest was increasingly demanding Achilles attention – winemaking. He had finally paid off the mortgage on the family home, and he had also met Clare, who would become his wife. Her parents had bought their dream home in the countryside, where they own a small vineyard and winery. Achilles rediscovered something he did as a child when he began to play an active part in the winery.

> I had always made wine with my father at home. He learnt the craft from his father, who was a vigneron in Greece. Then I was encouraged by my father-in-law to build on my traditional winemaking techniques through formal studies. So I returned to study wine science at night school. I love making things. Being able to create something from one natural source, getting a simple fruit, the humble grape, and helping it along to become wine. I'm intrigued by seeing it change state, and all the biochemical processes that are involved in its evolution into wine. This is where my interest in science is satisfied; here science meets art for me. I revel in being able to manipulate the process and in a way control the end result if

necessary. I aim to let nature take care of things as much as possible, as it has for 6,000 years – this is something big commercial wineries do not do. I consider my job is to be a caretaker of the wine's journey. I am fascinated to see the wine take on a life of its own as it changes state once again through the maturation process. And finally, I love seeing people drink and enjoy what I have made.

Beyond all that, winemaking is special to me because I feel wine's connection with the ancient world. Mediterranean civilizations have been built on the cultivation of vines, and my "Greekness" makes it somehow "in my blood". There is something about it that helps me express my ethnicity. Winemaking balances my creative aspirations and my scientific interests. Although being a mechanical engineer can be creative, after eighteen years it had lost that for me. My interests had moved far beyond electronics.

Achilles took time out to do more research into his new hobby, to experiment and see whether it could become a new career. While still in his job as a photocopier engineer, he took three months' long-service leave and spent the time making wine for a large Greek company. He combined the break with achieving his dream of travelling through the wine regions of France. Increasingly Achilles wanted to become recognised as a winemaker. He had entered his wines in amateur shows and was beginning to sell wine successfully. These small successes encouraged him to believe that he could be something other than a photocopier engineer.

For the first time I could see the possibilities of making a good living from something that I felt was creative and interesting. This would be the perfect job for me. Now that I'd found it I had to find the confidence in myself to make it become a reality.

It was "doing" which built up Achilles's confidence. Having started to immerse himself in this new world, contacts and opportunities began to come his way. A fellow student on a wine course he'd joined told him about a position at a wine distributor. The position had been empty for a few months and the company was looking for someone quickly. Achilles jumped at the chance of applying, but he hadn't had a job interview for eighteen years!

> The process of rewriting my CV made me realize how many transferable skills I actually have. Seeing what I had to offer on paper gave me confidence. It made it more real. Even though I had never been involved in the sales profession before I felt confident I had a lot of knowledge and experience to offer this company. "How hard could it be?" I said to myself. The rest I could learn. So I got an interview. This terrified me, but I went and bought a complete new suit. At least I looked great! We got along well instantly, which calmed me down, and within twenty minutes of finishing the interview they had called and offered me the position. It seemed too good to be true. It can't be this easy! I thought. Why had I waited for all these years? I think I had this almost effortless experience because the timing was right and I'd found a good match. Within one month of the interview I was in a completely new job for the first time in nearly nineteen years. It was surreal.

And with that Achilles got a job selling wine full time to restaurants for a major Australian family-owned wine company. He continues to be the winemaker for his in-laws' boutique winery, which is two hours north of Melbourne. Achilles hopes to be making and selling his own wine full time for the family business soon. But for now he is extremely happy just to be out of the world of photocopiers and successfully relaunched into an industry he loves.

Would he have done anything differently? His only regrets were not to clarify a few details with his new employer before accepting the job – just so that his expectations could have been clearer. Also, if he did it again, he would have taken a break between the old job and the new.

I finished my old job on a Friday and started the new job on the Monday. I didn't get the chance to reinvent myself. I think if I gave myself time to reflect on the past and come to some kind of closure my new role wouldn't have been such a big adjustment.

The biggest challenge for Achilles has been the worry of whether or not he could actually do the job. "Still, the only way of getting over my anxiousness was by getting on and doing it. Facing the fear and somehow believing in myself."

Achilles loves his new job but he is already tuning in to those aspects in his new career that he really enjoys. He's not going to sit back. He has a clear idea of where he wants his future to be. He does have down days when, as with his old job, he feels frustration that his creative potential is not being fully realized. So he tries to focus on the target of transferring his skills in selling other people's wine to eventually selling his own.

But there are other aspects to the job that he really enjoys.

I do a lot of staff training in my sales role. It involves teaching young waiters about wine. Often this is their first real close encounter with wine and I love seeing their interest ignited. This gives me a great sense of accomplishment, so much so that I am considering how my next business move can involve more of this kind of "education" work.

Few winemakers have the ability to make and market their own wine, so I've gained invaluable skills that will make me more of a "complete package". It was a good decision to work for a bigger company as an interim step, rather than go straight into freelance winemaking. This experience has given me the confidence to make the next step in my change.

In the last few years I have received some awards for my wines from various competitions. A highlight was receiving silver in Paris and

Brussels shows. This year I won a "trophy" (best wine in the class) for the first time. I was very proud of this result. I took it as a sign that I am ready to become a "fully fledged" winemaker. I needed no more convincing that I have what it takes. Now I am aiming to combine this success with the confidence I've gained in building relationships with restaurateurs. I now know that combining my ability to relate to people with my love of winemaking will be successful. By success I don't mean making loads of money, just enough to pay the bills. By success I mean doing what really interests me for a job. Although now I realize this might change in years to come, but that's OK.

ACHILLES'S ADVICE

1   Seeking professional advice can be helpful. I had counselling from a psychologist who helped me analyse why I was in a rut and helped me work on my self-confidence.

2   If you're feeling stuck, keeping your other enthusiasms alive beyond the workplace can help with ideas for a career change. Childhood passions can be a key to the future.

3   Making a major change is not like going from black to white but rather travelling slowly through greyness!

COUNTDOWN TO YOUR DREAM JOB
Carole Ann's career coaching boot camp

PROCRASTINATION

Sometimes we can mull a situation over and over to the point of freezing ourselves in analysis paralysis. The pros and cons lists cease to help, friends and family are sick of giving you free advice and hearing your "stuck-record" moaning, and even though you've forensically thought things through and studied every infinite possibility you find yourself still stuck at square one.

Procrastination may seem like the point of least resistance, but in reality it's agony, and the longer you mire yourself in doubt the more painful it becomes. In short it's fear-based behaviour; at the root lies something scary you don't want to face.

In coaching we work to help people get out of inertia and into action by setting small tasks, the "baby steps". We talk a lot about "doing" in this chapter, and action is the key. Energy begets energy, so every action and every step, no matter how small, is one closer to what you may be looking for.

In the "doing" you also learn that although it may feel counter-intuitive to leap in without analysing every detail, the pay-off is that it becomes strangely liberating, and caution turns into "I can".

> What can you do right now to move you one place nearer your dream job?
>
> Who do you know who might be able to help you in some way?
>
> What exactly are you waiting for?

CAROLE ANN'S ACTION PLAN

1. Get out of your head and start doing things. We can live in castles in the sky, but it doesn't get us anywhere. ACTION IS ALL.

2. Start being curious – explore evening classes, look in books, check out websites, research, make it as fun as possible, enjoy the process.

3. Keep the dream alive every day by doing something.

4. Check out www.scienceofgettingrich.net for sheer inspiration and off-the-wall motivation.

⑤ Remember, nothing is wasted – even things that don't work have shown you something.

⑥ Remember the here and now, though, and add polish, shine and value to everything you do (even in your day job) and with whoever you come across. It will pay off. Go the extra mile.

CHAPTER 6

REFLECTION

66 In life, you only get one chance. You can either make chicken s*** or chicken salad.[1]**99**

Carrying out the *doing* of the previous chapter will have brought about new insights and self-knowledge. Now is the time to fully internalize the new information you are acquiring. It may seem overwhelming, and perhaps you still lack clarity and no meaningful path is making itself known despite your best efforts.

Time to take stock and reflect. The busy-ness of this phase can often lead to burn-out. It's a common complaint of the career-changer that one reaches total exhaustion, trying to juggle the demands of the old world with the need to make explorations into the new. All this work and nothing to show for it. What's the point? Isn't it easier to accept the misery you are in rather than the dreadful "not knowing" all this journeying is bringing up?

Remember, finding a new job is often a full-time project in itself, and it won't happen immediately, as these stories show.

The rewards are high. A life and job you'll love will add meaning and purpose to all that you do. It's worth the search. Once the phase of *doing* gets under way you may quickly find a compelling new vision awaits you. If your exploration doesn't result in an immediate vocation or a quick new job opportunity, however, you may feel the time spent investigating is unproductive. Despair and despondency beckon.

GETTING REAL

It is entirely normal to go through the "brick wall" phase when you've tried everything and nothing is happening. Or so it seems. Nevertheless, behind the scenes in your psyche, plenty is going on.

You need to reflect on what has been going on. Ask yourself:

- What's working and not working for you?
- What do you know now that you didn't before?
- What part is fear playing in how you are feeling?
- Is your inner critic (*"You'll never do this. Nobody will want you"*) working overtime?
- Aren't you entitled to happiness and success?

It is important at this stage to acknowledge all the things you have learnt.

Everything you do now not only informs you but moves you farther away from your rut routine. You're on your way towards something new. This is thrilling stuff.

If you are looking for a major career change and have had no real direction, the reality is that it could take you one to two years – and far longer in some cases. Your first intentions may get dropped or you may come back to the same ideas repeatedly. While Patrick, from an earlier chapter, reassessed his future in a week, he had in fact been mulling over a change for years. Likewise Jenni, who seemingly handed her notice in "out of the blue", had actually been looking seriously for an alternative career for eighteen months and had been hoping for a change for seven years.

Allowing for this period of assessment and reflection is vital in defining what it is you find meaningful and enjoyable, what your priorities are, where your talents lie and what skills and experiences you need to acquire for a new future that you actually want. In the process of self-discovery, the job and lifestyle that will enable you to feel "more you" will become apparent. Finding time for reflection is a vital part of the process. A day off, a walk, a holiday, staring out of the window are all potential opportunities for the brain to find space for analysis and to have fun and be creative about the future. Deborah (Chapter 5) stared out of the window and conjured up a vision of her whole future business plan. The clarity with which ideas *can* arrive once out of the rut of routine is extremely gratifying!

 Life is an adventure or it is nothing.

In your search for the dream job, think about how you can make the process easy. You may be under the impression that life has to be a hard struggle and that nothing comes easily. You may well be incorporating this idea into your attitude to work – your own and other people's. You may well believe that anything worthwhile has to be like walking on broken glass.

If that's what you believe, then that's how it will be. But what if it's easy? What if you don't have to struggle? It could be that your future job is staring you in the face and you never thought of it as your "thing". Allow yourself to believe the possibility that you can earn money from something you already enjoy doing.

Perhaps you should make a choice – the choice not to struggle. You're going to play, have fun. When it becomes complicated, seek an easier route. Keep it simple.

Tanya was so convinced her dream would be a struggle and that she would fail. She gave up on it before she even tried!

✱ DREAM JOBBER

Tanya

Age: 30s

Was: Worker in NGO

Now: Journalist, South Africa

Key to success: Overcoming a fear of failure

Passion: Writing

What happens if you deny yourself the opportunity of fulfilling your potential? What happens if fear grips you by the throat and makes you stay put? You watch time merrily pass you by as you remain locked, trapped, too scared to pursue your dream.

Tanya knew exactly what her dream was – to be a journalist in her homeland, South Africa. But her fear of failure meant she was far too frightened to pursue it.

She found the perfect excuse not even to try. Johannesburg did not have a university with a journalism course, and her parents couldn't afford to send her away. She told herself, "I could have been a brilliant journalist, but ..."

Cue EXCUSES.

Instead, Tanya took a job working for a non-governmental organization. All worthwhile stuff, but it wasn't a full-time writing job. Instead she designed materials for workshops about conflict resolution.

In 1996, when South Africa was still recovering from the ravages of apartheid, I was delighted to be offered a job at an NGO in Cape Town. In the eyes of the world, the historical moment had come in 1994 with our first democratic election. But, for the vast majority of South Africans, this was just the symbolic beginning of a very long journey towards true liberation.

I knew that by working in the NGO sector, I could help with the immediate fall-out of what had happened here. Mine was not a world of policy, law-making or economic growth plans. It was, instead, a world where wise old women living in abject poverty were learning techniques for mediation and resolving conflict in their communities. Teenagers from under-resourced areas were becoming peer educators, while teachers were embracing the life skills that would give hope to the next generation.

It was all incredibly valuable, and often interesting, work. But it wasn't her dream. A minimal part of this job involved editing, and writing for, the in-house magazine. She focused on this small element of the job, which allowed her to write about some of the inspiring projects she'd worked on.

I was writing about a community gardens project, and I was interviewing a man in his seventies who had been given one of the small vegetable patches to tend. The context was the barren, desolate landscape of the Cape Flats in the Western Cape. This land, devoid of any natural greenery, was allocated to "people of colour" during apartheid. "In the morning," he said to me, "I wake up for those vegetables. Before, there was nothing to get up for. Now, when I think of my spinach and cabbage I must feed, I just kick the blankets off." His face lit up like a young boy's.

It was moments like these which confirmed for me how much I love hearing other people's stories, and then retelling them in the form of journalism where context, analysis and other perspectives can also be woven in.

Even this small opportunity to write gave her a thrill and ticked all the right boxes for her. But it still wasn't writing for a living, which Tanya knew was her calling. And eventually the rot set in.

> After two years at the NGO I realized it wasn't right. But, because I'm a cautious person, I didn't have the guts to leave there and then. I stuck it out by focusing on the positive, but eventually I realized I had to move on. Obviously, anyone with a conscience can get some pleasure working for an organization that's leading to some sort of development, but the results weren't immediate and I found that frustrating. What excited me more was when I wrote those articles and I got to put pen to paper and say this person was unemployed but now they grow vegetables.

> Also the culture of NGOs in South Africa was very slow, everything's so democratic! We'd have long meetings about team-building and other touchy-feely stuff. I wanted deadlines, adrenalin and an editor who wanted something by 3 p.m.! I really enjoyed the NGO work most of the time, I think it shaped me as a person and I met amazing people, but by and large my temperament wasn't cut out for it.

In spite of not having the temperament for it, Tanya sat it out for four years. But during this time she was obviously mulling over and reflecting on what elements of this job she liked, and what simply didn't suit her. In search of work that brought quicker results, she eventually ended the stagnation and went to work for another NGO. She lasted only two months.

> I thought, maybe pure training would be more satisfying. Training could be much more interactive and I would see the results of the workshop much more easily than if I'm just developing materials. But that was where I had my revelation that I was on the completely wrong path! On reflection, I realized I'd chosen pure training and no writing. When I first started working there I was so angry with myself for moving to a job I hated. I was a square peg in a round hole. It was

the first time in my life that I had bosses who didn't like me. It just didn't feel right.

Tanya had needed to make a move, any move, to get her out of the rut into which she was beginning to sink. By doing something different, she was able to analyse her new misery and draw conclusions. This new role made her unhappier because it took her farther away from the only element of her previous job she was beginning to really enjoy – writing. But, as ever with these "wrong moves", it proved for Tanya to be both "the biggest mistake and the biggest blessing".

> My boss called me in one day and said, "You seem very unhappy here. Your old colleagues talk about you as driven, chatty and charismatic. All I see is someone quiet, withdrawn and depressed. It's like we're talking about two different people." Although the move to the new job felt like the wrong move, if I hadn't made some change I might have stayed at the old job for ever. I had to go to a really terrible job before I could say, "OK, what do I want to do now?"

The new circumstances forced Tanya to really sit back and think about what she wanted. There were elements to the job she'd enjoyed – meeting people, entering different worlds, writing.

> Reflecting on that experience, I learnt that if you're happy in a job and challenged then you must stay there, but if you're only content in a job you must leave. Certainly for me, when I'm in a comfort zone, it's time to move on if I want to grow as a person. That has informed me in so many things since then. With me there is an overlap when I realize it's time to move on. But I dig my heels in a bit, and then I "hum" and "ha" about it and drive everyone mad in the process. You recognize that something is nice, but it's just too comfortable and not challenging and you have to get out. But actually if you stick it out it'll be because of fear, not because you're actually enjoying yourself any more. You're too scared to jump off that ship and on to another one.

The work at the NGO had been hugely rewarding. As Tanya assessed the past to inform her future, she knew that she wanted to work in a related field and be part of the reconstruction of the new South Africa. She had been inspired by the variety that was sometimes a part of her job. But she noted she was at her most dissatisfied when she had entire days and weeks sitting in the office. She hated being in the same place all day. She worked out that by pursuing journalism she would get more of what she loved without the stuff she hated. She mapped out a way to move forward.

> I experienced a eureka moment shortly after being called in by my boss. I was driving in the car and thinking about everything. I said to myself, "I know that I don't want to work there, I don't want to be a trainer, I don't want to work at an NGO. I still want to be a journalist!" It was a do-or-die situation. I could mope around in other jobs for the rest of my life or go after the thing that might satisfy me but which I was terrified of. I had to get to that point of reaching a cliff edge before making a decision.

Tanya handed in her notice. She cried profusely with relief. There were to be no more excuses, but these were also tears of anxiety for the unknown future. But while taking the decision to pursue a career in journalism was scary, being stuck for years to come in a job she hated had grown to be an even more frightening prospect.

> I applied to a university that only takes ten people for the course I wanted to do. I was afraid of being accepted! And then I got a letter saying I *had* been accepted. Then I said to myself, "Oh well, it's too expensive." (I still had those get-out clauses, but it was just fear talking.) Then my dad said I must follow my dreams and that he would pay for me to study again for a year without working. He said I was very lucky to have found the one thing that made me tick. It's true. I would have tried to be positive about all other jobs, but I was never going to be completely over the moon until I'd found

journalism. I was 27 by now, so it was quite a daunting prospect moving to a small university town where I knew nobody and finding I was a lot older than the other students. It was terrifying, but I sold all my things, packed up my car, and drove to the Eastern Cape eight hours away to begin my year of REALLY becoming a journalist.

Tanya had finally done it – jacked in a job that no longer fulfilled her and dared to pursue the dream she'd been denying herself. She came to realize that any other job would always be second best. Journalism fitted the brief that she had worked out she was looking for. And having finally made it into the journalism school and acclimatized to student life and communal living, did it work out?

Here was an opportunity to be whatever I wanted to be. I wasn't a daughter, a girlfriend or someone who worked for an NGO, I was just *me*. I learnt a lot about myself and that I could make friends even when surrounded only by strangers. The experience really highlighted both my strengths and weaknesses.

It was the most amazing year I've ever had, but it was also the most difficult. The lectures were amazing and as I sat there it felt like I'd come home. By doing this I'd hit the nail on the head and I knew that this was exactly what I was interested in. It had been such a gamble, but from the moment I got here I never doubted the choice I made. I handed in assignments and right from the start I rose to the top. It was just so natural for me to be doing it. I knew it was my passion, my calling. It was amazing – and clear, very quickly, that I was going to be good at this and that I'd found the right thing. I passed *cum laude*.

Once the course finished, Tanya returned home to Johannesburg and sat at home twiddling her thumbs with no job to go to. Beginning to panic, she applied for a subeditor job on the *Star*, a prestigious and widely circulated daily in South Africa. But it wasn't *writing*. After three weeks of hearing nothing she applied for a scholarship to do an MA in journalism. Within three days she was offered both. She couldn't choose between studying again and having a full-time job. So she did both!

What followed was an extraordinary year. In addition to her new job and studying, Tanya's father was diagnosed with cancer. She worked as a subeditor from seven until three and attended lectures from four until six. Working as a sub was far more exhausting than writing. She would then visit her father in the evenings. Her father's thirst for knowledge matched her own and he embarked on an MA in biography writing. She spent precious time with him, sharing his interests, and attended some of those lectures too.

If that weren't enough, Tanya was also writing her dissertation. "It was an absolutely exhausting year. But my dream was beginning to come true. I had a job in my chosen field and doing an MA was very satisfying." While it wasn't writing, the subediting job gave her work experience and a foot in the door. She learnt a lot about journalism and current events from that job. And in preparation for any writing posts in the future, she continued to build her CV and wrote articles in addition to the day job.

> It nearly killed me, but in one year I had worked full time and I completed my masters degree. I graduated two days before my father passed away. But he had left me the most precious gift of all – the freedom and courage to go back to my original dream of journalism.

While she was working as a subeditor, two writing posts on the paper were advertised, one on the culture page, and another in the newsroom. She admits that she still wasn't brave enough to take the bull by the horns and head straight to the newsroom. So she took what felt like a smaller leap by applying for the job she felt most comfortable with – that of culture correspondent. She knew a lot about film, music and the art scene. This was the moment in which Tanya had to prove herself in order to step inside the world of full-time and paid writing. After a good interview she was offered the job and began to settle in. She overcame her fear of being competitive and got into the groove of competition. She also began to offer up ideas for news-based stories to confront her fear of the newsroom.

> From the safe position of knowing it was not expected of me as part of my job as a culture writer, I would pitch news ideas about youth culture and subcultures to the main section of the newspaper. I kept going and I kept pushing. I had been too scared to go straight to the newsroom, but doing it this way I felt I could pitch ideas voluntarily without making a fool of myself.

After a year, she recognized the familiarity of a comfort zone beginning to materialize. But it took her another year to make a move. Having steadily built up her confidence over time, she applied for a job in the newsroom and was successful.

> Once in this job, when I had the confidence, I negotiated my job description to reflect what I knew I was good at. I didn't want front-page news. Shootings or riots excite some people, but they're not me. I'm more interested in talking to the families one week later and exploring the fall-out of the violence in South Africa.

So, after all her trepidation, here she was in the newsroom where backbiting and stamping on others were par for the course. How did she cope?

> I found that very difficult to swallow. But it's the price you pay to do something you love. Animosity towards me has never been overt, but I did experience the fiery competitiveness of the newsroom. And I think the bitching between subs and writers is probably universal.

She went on to become a senior journalist in the newsroom and is now the proud holder of two national and two international awards for her journalism.

Imagine if Tanya had remained locked in fear, missing out on having her perfect job and fulfilling her potential because she had continued to be too scared to pursue her dream. What a different story it would be. Still in a job she'd outgrown, increasingly miserable, beginning to bore her friends and family. Wouldn't you think that was a waste?

Having gone from a position of fear to fulfilment, what does she think of her own career move?

> It is amazing. I think the key to it is I have always actively worked on myself. At various stages in my life I've always done something to further myself. Looking back, when I didn't know what to do career-wise, I did courses outside work to make sure I didn't get stuck in the cushy comfort zone again. Because I have been there in the past – and I know what it leads to – I kept on learning. And then I found the guts to pursue what I really wanted to do. In my twenties I probably had the talent for writing, but never the courage to go for it.

Reflecting on her past proved a very powerful force in shaping her future. Tanya is a person who now initiates change in her life. She keeps moving, keeps stimulated, informed and fresh.

> After seven years I'd reached a dilemma. I had a young daughter and a great job but I was sick of Johannesburg. So, a year ago, I left the *Star*, and my husband, my daughter and myself moved to Cape Town. It was a gamble because I couldn't be sure there was enough freelance work, and I found it heartbreaking to leave a job I loved. But as it turns out there is plenty of freelance work, and I now choose very specific projects which give me the time to be very thorough in what I research and write. I applied for and was awarded a media fellowship and I am currently immersed in five features about child murders

and abuse in South Africa. Such projects allow me to really delve into the subject and cover the things in the way I want to cover them. I still see different worlds but can go into some depth rather than repeatedly writing one-off articles.

TANYA'S ADVICE

1 Completely identify what makes your heart sing. Not what your dad, your boyfriend or your friends think you should be doing. Find what inspires you. You will be so excited when you find that "thing".

2 Then, have a concrete game plan. Don't allow yourself to waver or deviate from it. Don't make excuses that it's not the right time, or say "I'll just do this in the meantime."

3 Just think of yourself lying on your deathbed one day. Would you rather say, "I spent another twenty years at my firm because I was too scared to make a move"? Or would you rather say, "I took a huge leap of faith and it was terrifying, but you only live once"?

And what would Tanya be doing instead if she hadn't found the courage to pursue her "calling"? After much hesitation she replied, "I simply cannot imagine doing anything else."

 Success = doing what you said you would with ease.

COUNTDOWN TO YOUR DREAM JOB
Carole Ann's career coaching boot camp

TRUST AND BELIEF

Anyone who has ever been on a diet will know that sooner or later you hit a plateau. You're all fired up and the weight is dropping off, your waistband is getting looser and you're even beginning to develop a taste for yogurt and steamed broccoli.

Then it all grinds to a halt. What you've been doing suddenly doesn't work any more. The scales stay put and you hit a wall of despondency. You can decide to throw in the towel and book a night in with a two-pound box of chocolates with a "what's the point?" sigh or you can take stock and reassess your strategy.

So it is when we start to pursue our big dreams. Excitement and optimism propel us forward in the beginning when it's all new and we feel energized. But how can we keep the faith and remain tenacious when one door slams shut and another refuses to open?

As you can see in this chapter, several times our storytellers recall that the goal often took them down circuitous routes and to places that didn't match their vision of where they wanted to be. In retrospect these "bends in the road" or "wrong turns" were still part of the journey.

CAROLE ANN'S ACTION PLAN

1. Think about the elements you want in a new working life, and the ones you want to eliminate.

2. Don't be put off by the pace of events, and don't panic if nothing clear and fixed appears immediately. Sift through your experiences, gleaning new information and allowing yourself time to fully internalize it.

3 When the time's right, resume the exploration of a possible new career rather than getting stuck. Don't give up. The really important thing is to maintain the momentum. Everything you do informs you and moves you further from your old role.

4 What might you be avoiding looking at that could be keeping you stuck? What place does fear play in your thinking at the moment? Think of something that feels easy and effortless and do it. Now!

5 Complete the following statement: "If I knew everything was going to turn out 100% in my favour I would .... right now."

6 Why not get hooked up with a buddy mentor? If you have a friend who is unhappy at work or has a goal they want to aim for, why not support each other and build in weekly telephone catch-up and brainstorming sessions or daily email check-ins? Accountability really sharpens the focus. Make sure the pal is a positive one, though. Remember, misery loves company.

7 Are you holding on to a negative belief that is scuppering your progress, such as "I don't deserve more money/a great job/acclaim" or "I knew this would happen – no doors opening, it's all right for them, I always struggle, life's always this difficult for me"? This is victim thinking and isn't helpful. It's time to reframe those thoughts, e.g. "I am going to succeed", "I will find what I'm looking for", "I choose to invest in myself", "I'm great and I deserve more". Our thoughts aren't real, but we do become them. Choose good, supportive ones.

8 Think deep here and be truthful. What might be the hidden pay-offs of being stuck/unhappy/blaming yourself at the moment? Revealing, isn't it?

CHAPTER 7

RESTRUCTURING

66 I tried lots of things – portrait painting, murals, illustration – and I could just about make a living, but it really wasn't going anywhere, and when I started to write, it really was like coming home. I had that feeling of, Oh, for God's sake, *this* is what I was supposed to be doing. And so the pleasure is in finding something you're good at. **99**

A. A. Gill (restaurant critic, UK)[1]

The time has come to make a further commitment to your career change and restructure your working life. You may want to decrease the number of hours you work. Or you may want to increase them. You do have a choice.

THE OPTIONS

- Arrange a career break or negotiate a period of unpaid leave
- Go part-time
- Get a second job
- Retrain
- Leave (including redundancy)

CAREER BREAKS OR UNPAID LEAVE

Taking a period of time out can be a vital part of the process of change. Sometimes it is the only way to fully break routine, recharge and gather strength to think about alternatives. If you are confined by an inward-looking job that brings no interaction with the outside world (you have no clients or companies to contact), then a structural change of some sort is even more essential to get out of that rut and engage with the world. Taking time out may complement the 'reflecting' process of Chapter 6. But don't forget to set a fixed period. It may be that you organize another period of time out later on – one to recharge, one to explore.

Kath

Kath had worked in the same company for fifteen years and she felt she needed time out. She successfully negotiated a career break of four months.

> When you want a change, people say "get another job", but I couldn't face that either. I wanted a change of routine and to leave the city.

During a meeting with her boss, as the planning of annual projects got under way she suddenly blurted out her plans for a career break. She knew she needed to get her own project into the timetable, otherwise the opportunity would disappear. Kath admits to being frightened of telling her boss for the simple reason that she knew this was the person who could stop her. Fortunately her boss was very supportive of the idea. While Kath was up for an open-ended holiday, however, her boss wanted it restricted to a finite period. They settled on four months. As it turned out it was just the right amount of time.

Something else to be prepared for is the deluge of work you may be assigned before leaving. Kath felt she was given an unreasonable amount of work to complete before her departure. This was coupled with time-consuming and stressful attempts to rent out her flat in order to help cover her mortgage for three months.

In preparation for the break, Kath had been learning French, and she remembers the day she committed to the idea and bought a one-way ticket to Paris, determined to get her French "out of the classroom and face the music". She knew Paris and had a friend there, but she was still frightened to death at the prospect of this self-imposed upheaval. This was coupled, however, with excitement at the thought of waking up to the unfamiliar.

> I had lived abroad before and I knew I could do it again. But when I arrived at the Gard du Nord, there I was, just a few hours from

London, but already it felt amazing. I had some savings, I didn't need much and I could work if necessary. At first, I spent a lot of time composing letters to museums and galleries because that's what I knew. But I didn't want to be in an air-conditioned office sitting next to people emailing all day. I went for an excruciating interview at the Pompidou Centre with a posh Frenchman. I can still see the mystified look on his face: he clearly couldn't make sense of what I was saying. It was a turning point when I realized that I just didn't have the level of French required. What was the French for "browser settings", "image resolution", "streaming videos"? After this rejection, to buoy up my flagging spirits I headed straight to the shops and bought a skirt from Cacherel. I instantly felt better. I walked into a restaurant I liked the look of and asked for a job. They took me on!

I spent a boiling hot summer sweating up and down the stairs, while they shouted at me as if I was an imbecile. I felt like Manuel in *Fawlty Towers*. It was a humbling, if masochistic, experience. I couldn't depend on status or language or friends. I had to act on the instant, be nice and be very clear about what I wanted to say. I was stripped away. Everything became simple and basic. I had just twelve garments and two books, but it meant I was self-sufficient, independent and not weighed down. It's energizing to feel so very different.

After the four months, Kath felt ready to come back to London and her much-missed friends and family.

But I returned to work feeling pleasantly detached. Even though I slotted back into exactly what I had been doing the day I left, I came back bolder and more confident. Same job, but I was a different person. When the possibility of a promotion came up as a producer, for once I felt very clear about what I had to offer. These positions were highly competitive and I had failed in the past. But I was objective, cold, detached. I had gained a perspective and everything had clarified in my mind. The interview proved easy and I surprised myself. Normally I would have rambled on, but I had spent the last few months having to be precise and economical with language. This clarity of expression came across in the interview and I don't believe I would have got that job without going away.

Kath has since been promoted to senior producer working on a range of engaging and demanding projects, including Ewan McGregor's motorcycle trip through Africa.

> If you're currently stuck, consider taking some time out. Work out what you are going to do and why. Don't worry about the how. And then work out what is stopping you. Have faith in yourself. You can escape any situation.
>
> Everyone can have their own personal revolution.
>
> A little bit of fear is good and a career break doesn't hurt. In the long term, it can be good to have people laughing at you in a language you don't understand!

Kath's promotion has provided the next adventure she was looking for. She's now engrossed in work she finds genuinely interesting, varied and challenging.

 TOP TIP The definition of luck – when preparedness meets opportunity.

GO PART-TIME

Going part-time can be an excellent way of restructuring your working life without jeopardizing everything. Anna used this method to distance herself from an office life she had begun to find stressful and to enable her to have time to research and write a book about sex. After years of strait-laced academia, she'd discovered it was this that she really enjoyed talking about.

Anna

Anna was a grade-A student who dreamt of winning a Nobel Prize by studying evolutionary biology at Cambridge. The dream came crashing down during a placement in a German laboratory, where she discovered she had little aptitude for practical lab work. Instead she underwent a crisis, re-emerging to pursue a career as an editor of a science magazine. It drew on her strengths – her ability to trawl through statistics, to be precise, to think logically, and to absorb information. In a team, that could be Anna's real contribution.

After working full time as an editor on the science magazine, she began to carry out her own research into a subject area that really fascinated her – sex. She started giving talks about sexual ethics. She recognized that she enjoyed discussing the issues of sex and fidelity in front of a curious audience. She felt that spirituality and sexuality were for her very much entwined. As her enthusiasm for the subject grew, she negotiated with her company to go part-time to give her the space to continue her research.

Going part-time enabled her to write a book, *Open Fidelity: The A–Z Guide*. Going part-time also taught her a lot about herself. And it proved to be a stepping stone before going completely freelance.

> I discovered I work better when I am my own boss. I am effectively running a business. I generate the work and I actually enjoy this far more than I expected. When the money arrives it means much more than the regular pay cheques of the past. This money doesn't just arrive, it's payment for hard-earned work which I've chosen to do! The work is growing, and this means I decide when I work and when I don't. I am no longer desperately taking anything. It also means I can take chunks of time out to write. I am currently writing a second book and a regular blog.

Having more freedom to plan her workload has enabled Anna to find a working life that suits her. Her new lifestyle has so many advantages over the old one. Much of her freelance work comes from the magazine she used to work for, but she enjoys the work far more now that she's not embroiled in office politics. She has the ability to create space to research and write. She gets paid more now than before and relishes running her business. In addition she's had time to get her book published and is really enjoying marketing and selling it.

But how does she reconcile this new editorial and writing career with the absence of the Nobel Prize she dreamt of as a child?

> The funny thing is that Nobel Prize-winners approached me asking to write articles for the science journal I was editing! I had status. I was more respected in that role than I ever was as a postdoctoral researcher. I've come to value time and freedom more than status and recognition. Although I'd like my book to become a best-seller, it is more important to me now to have a life and not just a career.

SECOND JOBS

Continuing with your full-time job does not preclude a job restructure. Getting a job in an area you think appeals in addition to your day job, while challenging, can be hugely rewarding. Pursuing what you really love outside work hours is a great way to (a) work out what you really love, and (b) alleviate the boredom of the day job. Project-managing your own adventures can help prove to yourself how capable you can be. Potential overlooked at work can be utilized elsewhere and is a great way of exploring a new future while maintaining a steady income. You may feel you don't have the strength, energy or willpower for two jobs, thank you very much. But doing something you enjoy in any "spare" time will be energizing and motivating.

Gemma

Over a gruelling twelve-month period, Gemma worked in two jobs in order to land the position of her dreams as a stylist for the UK's *Daily Mail*. During the day she did unpaid work experience at the paper, while in the evenings, in order to support herself, she worked as an assistant manager in a pizza restaurant.

> I was exhausted. My skin was terrible. But I was absolutely determined not to let go of the job at the *Mail*. I knew from the very first minute that this was what I wanted to do and I was determined to make it work. Fashion had been my obsession from a really young age. I'd go to the BBC's *Clothes Show* in Birmingham with my best friend and attempt to hang around in all the right places. I knew the names of designers, models and shops.

Opting not to go to university, Gemma initially worked at a fashionable high-street chain. While in this job, she got to know more about the roles available within the fashion industry and she got the chance to meet stylists who were working for clients and publications. "My friends in the shop began reducing their hours to go off and get experience in related areas. So I thought, OK, that's what I need to do. I too need to get some work experience."

She wrote to various newspapers and magazines, and the *Mail* wrote back and offered her a place.

> I was terrified. On the first day I was speechless. They had a fashion cupboard *full* of shoes. I was in awe, total shock and very nervous. They made me do the returns (i.e. sending the clothes back after a photo-shoot) for the whole week. I had no one to talk to. But I knew from the very first minute that this was what I wanted to do.

Gemma remained absolutely determined to stick at it and get herself a position. She did all the filing and the tedious jobs. But she also had to support herself by working in the restaurant. "It was incredibly demanding having to impress with this job I really wanted during the day and then doing another job in the evening."

When she was given a chance to prove herself at the *Mail*, she did. Within a few weeks of starting she was taken to a photo-shoot.

> I needed to prove that I was useful, I had to do it properly and be indispensable. Once I'd done that, people started to invite me on to shoots more often. By Christmas I thought, I'm here for ever. But it was a very stressful time. I had rent to pay and I'd work extra early in the mornings at the paper and then through till 11 p.m. at the pizza place.

The long hours were coupled with memorable challenges at the newspaper. In a *Devil Wears Prada* moment, Gemma recalls being faced with trying to find two hundred alarm clocks for a photo-shoot by 4 p.m. that afternoon. No store sold more than a hundred. A nail-biting last-minute delivery solved the problem … and then it was time to manage the restaurant! But her enthusiasm and hard work didn't go unnoticed by the fashion editor.

> I was given the opportunity of writing sidebars on the fashion pages: "Top 10 Bags", "Top 10 Blue Shoes" – that sort of thing. But I was still doing everything else. But I never complained. I did whatever was necessary to get the job done, and a contract and wages eventually followed.

After a testing twelve months, Gemma was finally able to relinquish the pizza job, having succeeded in being offered a paid role at the paper. But without that evening job she could never have afforded to follow her dream. Her commitment, conscientiousness and hard work were eventually rewarded with paid employment in the dream job.

RETRAIN

When entrenched in one job, retraining can be the opening to something new. Studying in your free time can get you experience and qualifications in a fresh area you otherwise don't have access to. It enables you to start meeting contacts within a new field you might want to transfer to.

Jason II

This Jason had a desk job in an insurance office in Liverpool, where he worked for six years. He never associated work with fun and he spent his life living for the weekends.

> I had a high-stress job in insurance that made me sick to the stomach some days. I worked in an open-plan office with 200 to a floor. The phones would ring with irate people complaining. The wage was crap, but I had a high level of responsibility. I lost the company a significant amount of money – it was partly my fault, but the buck stopped with me. At that point I *really* wanted to leave. But I didn't know where I wanted to be. I just got my head down and worked through it. But I was bored, going completely brain dead not knowing what to do as a career.

By chance, he was lent a book, *An Interview with the Vampire*, by Anne Rice. It was a small thing, but went on to have huge consequences.

> I never normally used to read and this book really caught my imagination. I was totally transfixed by the story and the writing. It kick-started a passion for reading and I became an immediate bookworm, soaking up everything and joining book clubs.

This was Jason's "ah-ha" moment, which proved to be his turning point. He started to read voraciously and in turn it renewed his interest in education. As a consequence, it led him on to a path of retraining that gave him direction and a route out of the insurance office.

> While still working at the insurance office, I embarked on a night school course in English literature. I then proceeded to a combined honours degree in psychology and fine art. Psychology because of my experience of the workplace, fine art because I used to enjoy art back in school. I was really scared and sick to the stomach, as I didn't really think I was capable of doing this. But I took courage from my other friends who had gone on to do degrees too, and I just thought if they can do it, I probably can too.

Jason believes his biggest challenge is himself. He constantly has to convince himself he can do things. He needed to convince himself he was capable of doing a degree. But immediately he started the course, he flourished.

> The first six months of the degree in fine art changed my life and it became my real interest. After graduating in a combined degree, art became my obsession. It proved a busy time. I returned to the insurance office, because it was an easy job as the stress was gone, and the money was good. I started to sell artwork and I also set up a business painting murals, which got me press coverage but meant I was working seven days a week. It was an intense and exhausting phase.

> During this period the university contacted me to say they were looking for a researcher and artist in residence. I went for the interview and I got the job – not because of my art only, but because I'd worked with statistics at the insurance office! So it goes to prove that no experience is wasted. I am currently the Fine Art and Design Senior Assistant and curator of a gallery in Liverpool. I am also a professional artist, having exhibited nationally and internationally. Ten years ago I never thought I'd be where I am now. I can't believe I've gone from an insurance office to being comfortable calling myself

an artist and running a gallery. Although it's very demanding and too much sometimes, I love my job!

Jason II discovered a whole new world when he re-entered education, one that revived an interest in art that he'd had as a child. His life was transformed. His potential as an artist would have remained totally untapped if he hadn't found the courage to explore interests beyond the office and eventually retrain.

LEAVE

There may be no other option for you but to leave your job. You may have fantasized endlessly about handing in your notice. But before you do it, bear in mind you may want a reference, or contacts, or freelance work, or friends and future customers. So think about *how* you leave. Many interviewees have voiced certain regrets about not keeping in touch, not networking, or being consumed by bad feeling towards the company they left. On the other hand there are those who never looked back.

What happens if you've been made redundant? Although not always welcome, redundancy is a way for your working life to be restructured. The trauma of enforced redundancy contrasts with the feeling of liberation for those brave enough to accept it when offered. Either way it's great to hear about the survivors: the city couple who got sacked and took the opportunity to set up their own cheese shop; the redundant magazine editor who set up a business selling carpets; the agent who, when made redundant, decided to go it alone, taking her hard-won clients with her; a radio continuity announcer who gave it all up to set up a painting and decorating company. They are all successfully up and running. Worry, and even torment, can accompany radical change, but, in hindsight, it's often the best thing that could ever happen.

So let's start with enforced redundancy, an often shocking, debilitating experience that crushes the self-esteem. Some of my interviewees who've been forced into redundancy have described themselves as feeling "humiliated", "betrayed", "old", "angry", "of no use", "devastated", "conned". But those who chose voluntary redundancy have described it as "liberating", "daunting", "challenging", "frightening", "fantastic".

Many of those I spoke to talked about the loss of confidence regardless of whether their redundancy was enforced or not. Receiving rejection letters from a position of unemployment lowers the self-esteem. Even if we feel that we are not defined by our jobs, much of our self-worth is still tied up with our occupations. Being made redundant will affect your confidence, and it may not be restored until another employer has shown their faith in you. Dealing with the aftermath of redundancy is not easy or straightforward, but it can be an opportunity.

Chris managed to turn his crushing circumstances around to enable him to have a most extraordinary adventure.

* DREAM JOBBER

Chris

Age: 44

Was: Lorry driver, UK

Now: Published author, UK

Key to success: Turned something demoralizing into an opportunity

Passions: Writing, travel, exercise

Chris is someone who made the best of his situation when his life was dramatically restructured. First, a long-term relationship ended and then he was made redundant, out of the blue. He was utterly demoralized.

If you found yourself in this situation what do you imagine *you* would do? Crawl under the duvet feeling worthless, worried and desperate? That's one approach, but Chris eventually decided to get himself together and capitalize on his new-found freedom. Incredibly, he decided to cycle across two continents and thirteen countries and pedal 16,500 miles! He cycled from his home in Worcestershire, England, to Beijing, China. It was the most extraordinary experience of his life – so far! That's an impressive way to deal with compulsory redundancy. How did he do it?

> Being told you are redundant is awful. To me it meant useless, surplus to requirements and inadequate. I was devastated by these two events in my life and I needed to do something to regain my self-respect, so I looked at my situation. In one way, the good thing was that suddenly I no longer had these commitments and obligations in my life. I didn't have children like many of my friends, so I was free. Here was an opportunity to do something. Could I seize it and turn something negative into a positive experience? I needed to prove that I wasn't useless. I began to think if I could turn this around I would regain my confidence. I decided I would seize the opportunity and do something remarkable. I always cycled to work, as travelling by train was so unreliable and I was passionate about exercise. When I drove in the lorry I always took my running gear; exercise was always at the back of my mind. It was at this point that I decided to take a bike trip.

But it was no routine bike trip. How did it come to this? If we go back a little we can begin to see how Chris reached his astonishing decision.

Chris was fascinated by transport from the age of five and his classroom at school overlooked the motorway. This was combined with a love of globes and maps. At fourteen, he was hugely excited by stepping on to French soil on a school trip. He became good at French ("lousy at everything else") and went on to graduate with a French degree.

At this stage, like many people, Chris had a clear idea what he didn't want to do. He didn't want a desk job and he didn't want to teach. So he indulged his enthusiasm for transport and got his Class I licence and a job as a long-distance lorry driver. In his truck, he travelled all over Europe, as well as to Russia and Kazakhstan. On Christmas Day, when his lorry broke down near Moscow, he was exhilarated by the fact he was fulfilling his childhood dream: "Even broken down, I wouldn't want to be anywhere else. I enjoyed what I did so much, getting paid was a bonus." To capture the adventures and extraordinary sights he was seeing, he started to keep a diary of travel notes. It sowed the seeds for his passion for writing.

Chris eventually reached the stage where he felt he had taken it as far as he could go. "I'd seen Kazakhstan in every season, I'd even seen camels in the snow." He decided the time was right to switch to a nine-to-five office job which would free up his weekends to develop his new-found love of writing. In his spare time, he developed a book idea and sent it to several publishers, but was rejected. Yet he knew he had some terrific stories about his travels, and through practising he was getting better at the mechanics of writing.

He secured a new job in the lorry company's office and just as he was settling in he lost both his girlfriend and his job.

Having picked himself up off the floor and decided to turn this negative situation into a positive one, Chris began to plan the cycle ride of his life. He pinned road maps to walls and started plotting his route. Physically, this would be the most punishing challenge, and he began training for the 80-mile-a-day journey. It would take an estimated eighteen months, working a route through Europe, the Middle East and India to his intended destination of Vladivostok.

After a glorious send-off, he set off on his momentous journey in May, but nearly ran aground immediately when he sustained an injury in France. He braced himself for a humiliating return home, but his French, and a local doctor, helped him on his way, and so his journey of a lifetime truly began. [Find out more about this astonishing journey on Chris's website, www.cycleuktochina.com]

After a gruelling cycle ride across China, he spent one week negotiating for a visa to get him to his hoped-for destination in Russia. He was devastated when the Russians refused him entry. He returned from his life-changing adventure (by aeroplane) with a book to write.

Unfortunately, he also faced debts and he therefore needed a job, quickly. So he went back to lorry driving. But he didn't let his ambition of writing his story slip. He religiously restructured his working life and set himself a daily regime of writing from 5.30 a.m. before cycling the thirteen miles to work each day. He was absolutely unwavering in his determination to complete his book. "In order to be successful at what you do," he says, "you have to love it. I love writing, although I have come to it late. I get a feeling of total exaltation when I get a phrase just right!"

The job loss was unwelcome – but it led to the creation of something fabulous. His incredible journey to Beijing is now in paperback and in the shops. Both the trip and writing the book have been an arduous but worthwhile struggle.

Occasionally Chris has crises of confidence, but knows they will pass. "Words don't sparkle when you're tired," he says. At the moment, promoting his book, *Why Don't You Fly?*, has replaced the writing. And slotted around the day job are the interviews, talks and book signings involved in the launch of the book. The fantastic news is, it's not only on the bookshelves, but it's also selling! (See 'Further Reading', page 214.)

Chris dealt with his redundancy in a truly individual and spectacular way. He managed to salvage a potentially soul-destroying experience, and he not only went on to make a dream come true, but in the process found material for his new passion of writing. He showed his commitment to this new vocation by restructuring his working life and writing in the early hours before work. For him, the publication of his first book was a major stepping stone towards his ambition of writing for a living full time.

CHRIS'S ADVICE

1   I don't regard myself as particularly talented or untalented, but I've refused to give up and take no for an answer.

2   Not having a passion is the worst position to be in. Everyone has dreams – but people give up on them.

3   You have to identify what it is you want to do. If you're passionate about it, you'll find the courage and conviction to carry it through.

RESTRUCTURE YOUR WORKING LIFE

Which is the most realistic option for you to get to your dream job? Can you begin the conversations to realize this aim?

Restructuring your working life, in whatever form, is a really useful way to explore new options, develop new talents and discover existing ones. Time out allows the opportunity for a recharge and a rethink. Taking on additional jobs and retraining allow you to experiment in completely new fields. They're also ways of finding out what's really important to you. You may discover it's quite different from what you had imagined.

 Before sacrificing everything, try it on first.

COUNTDOWN TO YOUR DREAM JOB
Carole Ann's career coaching boot camp

CH-CH-CHANGES

Human beings are creatures of habit. We are nothing but a complex series of them, from our morning grooming routines to what we eat and read; we follow self-constructed patterns every day.

This is why we all distrust change. It feels uncomfortable, we are suspicious of it, cynical and afraid; in some instances, because of its unfamiliarity, we feel challenged by it. But as we all know, change and new experiences soon become routine and then just another "habit" we unconsciously process every day. Just think how scary it is when you first learn to drive a car. You think you will never get the hang of it. As a practised driver you effortlessly and unconsciously know how to drive without having to refer to an instructor or manual.

The levels of learning are:

Unconscious incompetence – you don't know or think about how to drive a car.

Conscious incompetence – you are learning, but still aren't able to drive a car.

Conscious competence – you now know what it takes to drive the car and can do it.

Unconscious competence – you drive the car without thinking about it.

Eventually we all move into unconscious competence when the changes become so familiar we don't even have to think about them.

With that in mind, "change" becomes less of a threat and something you have to learn to ride through, and then familiarity leads to mastery.

Some of you may find you don't need a huge change in your career, and maybe going part time, taking up an absorbing hobby or moneymaking sideline or immersing yourself in something you are passionate about could be enough in itself.

Sometimes just cutting back on what you don't like and bringing in more of what you do can be sufficient to make you content, and a full life change or career switch may not always be necessary.

CAROLE ANN'S ACTION PLAN

1 Ask yourself, what do I need right now? Be very clear what you hope to achieve by going part time or what elements you are looking for in an additional sideline. Use this as a chance to have fun, do something exciting, challenge yourself and get back any flagging self-esteem! Prove what you can do.

2 If you need an extra job for financial reasons, it's time to weigh up the investment of time and energy involved – e.g., if you want to write a

book, is working in a pub until midnight each evening conducive to your creative flow and energy?

3 Seek advice on what you are entitled to legally at work for a career break or part-time status. Ask others who have done it what they got out of it.

CHAPTER 8

IMMERSION

❝More than 70,000 people spent part of Christmas or Boxing Day surfing for a new employer in an attempt to beat the competition … most persuade themselves to stay in unfulfilling roles because of fear.[1]**❞**

With the restructure of your life now in place, the next step is to immerse yourself in the world you want to become part of.

But how to get there? If you're working as an accountant, how do you build up contacts to become a stand-up comedian? If you've written a book, but know no one in publishing, how do you break through and get your potential best-seller on the bookshelves?

I'd written a book and knew no one in publishing. I continued to read books about getting published, writers on writing, newspapers and relevant feature columns. I could do all that on my own, and I became much more informed about the industry. But it was still me on my own, and a big gulf between me and the world I wanted to get to.

I began to talk about my book, and the moment I mentioned it, people seemed interested in its theme. Admittedly these were friends forced to show an interest – but it transpired quickly that while *I* didn't know anyone in publishing, other people did. Not only that, but they were very helpful. Tips and information began to come my way. These led to other conversations and phone calls with complete strangers. Emails and meetings followed. I'd gone from a complete impasse to a meeting every week with publishers.

It was all such fun, too – nerve-racking at first, but ultimately hugely enjoyable and informative. The barriers began to fall away and I suddenly had open access. I no longer had to devote time to sending proposals and being rejected by people I didn't know. I could now be turned down in person! Most often, people were busy but upbeat, and even if they were not the "right publisher", I always left with a new lead. It eventually led to a meeting with a publisher who was willing to take a risk and give a first-time writer a go.

Whatever your new, hoped-for arena, you need to find out about the relevant events, people and places to go to. What is it you can do on your own? Do your friends know what you're doing? How can they help? With the research you have done and steps you have already taken, some of this information will have materialized. There will be new contacts and perhaps some preliminary conversations. The more you read and talk to people, the better informed you'll be. You need to know how your new world works, what's needed, gaps in the market and any job opportunities.

At first, I paid for contacts. I paid a literary consultant to give advice on my book and have conversations with the publishers and agents she knew. Her advice was excellent, but the contacts never materialized. I actually found the free advice I received later from people in publishing more valuable. I attended events for writers, heard from literary agents and publishers and began to understand their position and their "slush" piles. With a book published every thirty seconds, my pitch really needed to convince and stand out.

IMMERSE YOURSELF IN YOUR CHOSEN FIELD

- What can you join, read, research or attend?
- Where can you find the people in your new arena?
- How can you get access to events? Could you stage one yourself?
- Can you blog or are there specialist websites to advertise or make contacts through?
- Who do you know who may be able to help you?

TOP TIP You have nothing to fear but fear itself.

Brigitte was another such person locked in one treadmill existence with no notion of how to get into or make contacts in her chosen, more appealing world. She needed to make connections, build those bridges and get the doors to her new career open.

✳ DREAM JOBBER

Brigitte

Age: 37

Was: Economics student, Denmark

Now: Professional singer

Key to success: Realization that life is short and valuable

Passion: Music

Brigitte is someone who did what was sensible for the day job, keeping her real passion on the fringes because she didn't believe she could earn a living from doing her dream job. After all, work's about being safe, secure and bored, isn't it?

Brigitte is a professional singer. She has secured a record deal and recently released her debut CD, but there was a time when such an idea was unthinkable. She qualified in economics and business – she did the "correct" thing. Like many of us, Brigitte had yet to realize that, as she puts it, we are "masters of our own experience". One thing she did realize, however, was that she was bored and she knew for certain that "life is too short to be bored".

She was born in Seville to a Spanish father and a Peruvian mother, but her father died at 37 when she was only eight. As you can imagine, this had a major impact on Brigitte, both instantly and on her subsequent approach to life. Time is limited, and therefore whatever she is doing must feel worthwhile. For her, this means following a life of integrity. While she'd be happy if someone offered her heaps of money, no one has so far!

> There's no value in dying with three million in the bank. It makes for a rich corpse, but it is not a massively attractive way to live if it means a lifetime of mindless dreariness.

The upheaval that followed her father's death included moving to Denmark, which became Brigitte's home for the next eighteen years. There, at the age of eleven, she started listening to music, became fascinated by it and realized it was for her. She became obsessed with the Beatles and began to teach herself a range of instruments, including guitar and piano. At a local youth club she watched someone else play. She didn't have the courage to speak, but would rush home to imitate what she'd heard. The Beatles also inspired her to learn English.

On the assumption that she was not a musical genius, however, Brigitte continued with the "safer" option and went on to complete an economics and business degree, keeping music as a hobby. She simply didn't have the courage to pursue her dream. But a fellow student, who was a professional singer, made her think twice about the decision she'd made. She discovered that her friend, although a professional, was still having voice lessons. It was a defining moment.

> It clicked for me. I realized that people are not necessarily born musical geniuses (though a few may be) and that I too could take lessons and improve. If this girl had got there by having lessons and working at it, then so could I. Until this point I had always been told

that to become a musician one had to be born a genius. I told myself I needed to be like Mozart, and if I had not written a symphony by the age of six then clearly it wasn't meant to be! But even Mozart, or should I say *especially* Mozart, had encouragement, teachers and support. I realized *that* was what I lacked. I set out to get it. I found a voice coach and started having lessons.

She became increasingly convinced that, with focus and hard work, music could become a realistic profession and a way of earning a living. Music shifted from being a sideline to becoming her main focus. Although qualified in economics and business, she signed up for a singing course. To fund herself she cleaned in a music school at night, went to college in the day and spent all her spare time practising.

After my father died, it dawned on me that in life there are no guarantees. Everything can be lost in an instant, so I saw no need to play it safe. I might as well make the most of my time here. To me, that means following my heart.

Having begun a course and organized training, Brigitte needed to make the next move and start finding contacts and a way into her new world. While there were possibilities in Denmark, she felt that England might provide her with greater opportunities. She made a huge transition in pursuit of her goal and settled in Manchester.

One thing she could do easily and without contacts was to start attending gigs in Manchester. She then began to organize her own gigs. She started performing at them herself. It gave her a sense of satisfaction and pride. "Every gig is exciting because it is different." The audience was made up of people like herself – passionate about music. She began to get to know the circuit and be known herself. She became part of a community of like-minded musicians, and she built up a network of new friends in the music scene.

A career in music was becoming a possibility. She lived and breathed the music scene and completely immersed herself in it. It took two years of hard work and performing. But eventually, one evening, she was spotted, and signed to a record label by a friend of a friend. This resulted in her debut CD. It led to being signed by Red Kite Records. But Brigitte admits that even with the dream of a record deal secured, it's hard.

> I'm 37 years old and life is short and valuable, but I've followed my dream, doing things I believe are right for me. My finances are precarious, I have no pension and I'm certainly not loaded! I perform regular gigs, but I also do some teaching in order to keep going – and it can be enjoyable. At certain times of the year I attend jazz festivals, and weddings, and the international work I get is great experience. It's also easier. In England the driving and travelling to venues late at night really isn't very glamorous. Sometimes, when there's not much work, it's difficult to plan for the future. I had a UK tour of the CD, but the musicians and pianist I played with were new to me, and then there was three months of no work, no monthly income, no colleagues. That can be difficult.

Because of the financial uncertainty of a singing career, Brigitte has contemplated getting an office job. But she has ruled it out. "It wouldn't be right for me."

> I taught in a college once, but there was no one-to-one time, just plenty of paperwork. It wasn't valuable, either for the children or for me, so it didn't feel right to do it. But it was a very useful experience, because I subsequently put more energy into finding gigs and getting more work of the kind I wanted.

Following a car accident, Brigitte suddenly faced the reality that she might never sing again. Instead of resigning herself to the thought of work she knew would not suit her, she worked out what she could do that would also be enjoyable.

> The worst experience was the car crash, because it led to laryngitis, of all things! I couldn't talk for six weeks, let alone sing. I couldn't work and I couldn't pay any bills. Jaw problems developed and I was diagnosed with arthritis.

It was a huge shock. Faced with the prospect of not being able to sing for a living, Brigitte knew she had to be resourceful and come up with Plan B. She decided she would paint and teach the piano. After all, she had painted up to the age of fifteen, and she believes that "creativity will come out, one way or another".

Luckily, she recovered her health, but she now knows she has the reassurance of a fall-back plan should she ever need it. She continues to perform and teach music on a one-to-one basis. She finds both equally rewarding and she loves the variety and the fact that every week is different.

> I get a sense of pride and satisfaction from the work that I do. Every gig is different. I'm doing what I feel I was put on the planet to do. Also I find there is satisfaction in teaching privately and passing on what I have learnt. You get a small voice and you watch it grow. It's very exciting. It's helping people to achieve their dreams and goals.

Along with the record deal, her highlights have included touring in Iceland, and being invited to sing for the UN Secretary-General and at the UEFA Cup Final in Milan.

Brigitte took a series of logical steps in order to make the transition from the business world to the music industry. First, to believe it was possible for her, she needed to see someone else living that dream. Then she totally immersed herself in her new world, training, practising, listening to music, attending gigs. She actually moved country in search of the British music scene. By interacting with the world she wanted to join and then performing herself, she became a familiar face and someone with friends and new contacts. "Making money was never a motivation for me. Enjoying life is my main aim. Having said that, business is good and I can afford to work when I choose to."

It's a great position to be in.

BRIGITTE'S ADVICE

1   Immerse yourself in a world that you find worthwhile. Find out what your passions are. Not everyone knows, but, in my view, we are put on this planet for a purpose.

2   The trick is to live the best way possible.

3   You have a choice of how you live your life. Living a safe life with routine and job security out of fear and not out of love is totally different to doing something you love. Once you're gone, what use will it have been? We're all headed the same way. What will you regret on your deathbed?

Good question. What *will* you regret on your deathbed? Why wait till then – what do you regret now?

 Dare to dream.

High-flying Ayu managed to succeed in a highly competitive media job, in spite of having trained in something else. She did it by immersing herself in this new field. She needed to know her subject in order to survive.

✳ DREAM JOBBER

Ayu

Age: 25

Was: Public relations student, Indonesia

Now: TV reporter, Indonesia

Key to success: Doing the best job possible

Passions: Music, reporting

Inexperienced and unqualified, Ayu managed to persuade an interview panel that she would be the best candidate for the job. Having achieved that, she had to live up to their expectations on a daily basis.

Ayu is an Indonesian television reporter and she lives and works in Jakarta. Such is her professional approach to work she will do whatever is necessary to get a job done. That may include working long hours, contacting the best people for the job, standing out in all weathers and ultimately, every time, trying to generate the best programme possible.

She adores her job as a reporter for RCTI, one of the biggest private television stations in Indonesia. Thanks to her dedication, she has been given opportunities to develop and progress. In spite of not having a broadcasting qualification, she has been successful in her chosen career because of her high standards and love of the work that she does.

Ayu openly admits to being fully immersed in her work and cannot wait to get started in the morning. She describes how her job makes her feel.

> Wonderful, complete, meaningful, imaginative. On a good day my job makes me feel *alive*. Because it is my life. I spend most of my time

working, more than being with family and friends. What I love most about my job is the fact that I can share great news that might be important to Indonesian people and help them in some way. It just gives my work meaning.

For example, yesterday I covered a court session about censorship. Some scenes have been cut from certain Indonesian films and the film-makers were contesting it. They felt that the particular cuts were arbitrary and, anyway, they believe there should be no censorship. If the film-makers win, it will have a big impact. And if they don't, it will still be part of the history of the Indonesian film industry. It's a great story and I love the fact that I can be there and bring the news to everyone.

But Ayu didn't start out wanting to be in television, or even to be a reporter.

I graduated from a three-year diploma in public relations and before that I freelanced in different places and worked as an event organizer. I wanted to be able to have good relations with people and businesses. I tried to find a job in PR, but there were no jobs going at that time. In the past five years the media has become very big here. There are eight private national television stations, many local television stations, several newspapers, tabloids and magazines, websites and radio. So, this is a popular area and many people want to be in it and study broadcasting at college. So I applied for a job as a production assistant at an international media company making television programmes.

When they interviewed me, I said, "I know there are many other people who might be smarter than me, but you won't regret it if you hire me because I like to learn everything and I will try to give my best for the company."

She knew she was entering a highly competitive field, but she pre-empted that competition by demonstrating her genuine enthusiasm for the job at the interview. She was open and honest about how committed she would be. They hired her. They didn't regret their decision.

Ayu had entered an unfamiliar field, but she proved she was willing to do anything. Having experienced the media, she knew this was where she wanted to be rather than pursue her original ambition in PR. She demonstrates just how far you can get and how successful you can be if you immerse yourself wholeheartedly in the work that you do. Volunteering for everything meant she gathered vital experience across a range of jobs, working on TV programmes like *Family Feud*, *Touch the Car* and *Indonesian Idol*. It proved to be essential preparation for the future and put her in a much stronger position when she decided to move on.

After two years, she began to look elsewhere to develop her career. The company had a limited range of programmes, which began to restrict her progress. In search of broader experience, she approached Indonesian television company RCTI.

> It is very difficult to be an RCTI employee because it has had a high reputation since it started eighteen years ago as the first private television station in Indonesia. Nowadays it doesn't even advertise jobs. Instead, they headhunt – perhaps from another television station, or perhaps someone gets lucky. I consider myself to be one of the ones who "got lucky". Actually, I sent my application by post six times in six months, just trying my luck in the hope that maybe they'd notice me. Eventually, they asked me to come for an interview and they showed me they had kept all my application forms. I had demonstrated to them that I wanted a job and that I was determined to get one. I had an interview and numerous health and psychology tests and had to answer ten questions about what I would do on the programmes. Then, finally, they offered me a job as a production assistant and it's just like a dream come true.

She went on to prove herself once again. Her performance was noticed and suitably rewarded.

> My manager asked to see me. Then he said that over the past six months he'd seen my skills, the loyalty and the efforts I'd gone to for the company. He said he wanted to give me an opportunity because he could see me grow and develop better if I became a reporter. I didn't have any qualifications for this job, but felt I could survive, so I accepted. Immersing myself in the job and being willing to do many jobs enabled me to get a wide range of experiences. So I think that's what made my boss feel he could trust me to be a reporter.

Some of her colleagues were less than happy, and Ayu really had to demonstrate that she warranted this chance.

> It was tough in the first month. Many people were wondering why I should be made a reporter and doubted my skills. I knew I had to try. My mum and boss believed in me so I didn't listen to any comments. On one occasion I made a mistake and couldn't remember the name of the person I had gone to interview. From then on I knew I had to be the best at my job and work really hard to be across everything. I focused on just managing myself and not turning into the failure they thought I would be. To start with, I asked many senior colleagues how to get information and contacts. I learnt from them until finally I could do it myself. While my colleagues were sceptical about me at the beginning, I took it in the spirit of being able to show them and prove that I could be a great reporter and my boss hadn't been wrong in giving this opportunity to me.

Not everyone operates like Ayu. She sees some people do their job half-heartedly, and there are others who want to spend more time with their families. But Ayu admits to living and breathing her job. Whenever her company needs help – even on a day off – she will come in, and always tries to be available. "I never clock-watch," she says, "I just do it." It's not simply the amount of time she spends at work: she feels she needs to know everything about news and current affairs events. To be the professional she is and do the best that she can, she is completely engaged in her work.

> A reporter must have a curiosity for all types of news, and I think I have had that since I was a teenager. A top reporter must also have a wide and broad general knowledge. That's something I'm still working on every day. The biggest challenge is feeling you have to know everything, more than anyone else. It makes me have to read, open my eyes wide, listen to every piece of information carefully and learn more and more. But I love it ...

> Every day my work has the same pattern. I come to the office, check the Internet for the latest news, read the newspapers, call some people who could possibly have great information. Then I'll call a cameraman (if I'm working with a partner) and a driver to go to an event. And my phone is always ringing. Some people say I work too much and that I'm crazy to work so late. But I don't feel that way!

Recently she has learnt to be a video journalist. This has broadened her skills, as she continually seeks to learn on the job and take up new opportunities. Her openness to opportunities means she is becoming better trained and increasingly indispensable as she accumulates a broad range of skills.

What really motivates Ayu? Talking to her, she doesn't come across as a pushy, ruthless person driven by naked ambition and drive. When I ask her about what encourages her, she says it's a desire to make her parents happy, to give of her best each day. And her religion motivates her and makes her embrace her job fully.

> I think I'm a success in terms of whether I can make my parents happy, because I saw them suffer a lot. I don't know if they're already happy with what I am now or not, but I think they know I always try my best in everything. My parents didn't have high expectations of

me. In fact, they never ask anything of me. They always say that it is enough for them if they can see me successful and happy. They didn't have much money to afford a house. So, from when I was born until now I have lived in different rented houses. Now I live in a rented house near my office, but I dream of buying a house for my parents someday. I always try to give my best no matter what and do my work with all of my soul. Facing my life in the mornings, I want to give the very best of me to others. In my religion [Islam], it is said that working is one way of getting closer to God's love. Sometimes I just feel I have so much energy inside.

Relations with colleagues are better now she has proved herself, and that's a vital part of the job. She needs to be part of a team and cooperative with the people around her to do the job properly. On a recent assignment covering the Miss World competition in China, they lacked a cameraman owing to numerous stories erupting across the country. "So colleagues taught me how to operate the camera and also how to edit pictures using a notebook, for two weeks, twelve hours a day!"

As a young employee, new and inexperienced in a competitive industry, Ayu is using her time wisely. But there are tactics she has applied that make her stand out from the competition – things we can apply to our own situations.

She sent in her CV *six times* to a company she really wanted to work for. She never gave up. Eventually she got the invite she was aiming for.

Her openness to opportunities and her willingness to do anything have enabled her to build up essential skills and catch up with her more experienced and qualified colleagues. She proves that enthusiasm and passion for your subject can make up for a lack of qualifications.

She messed up and had to take flak from colleagues, but she didn't give in and instead rose to the challenge and worked harder to prove herself as a new reporter. She wasn't going to get this opportunity again. She absorbed everything related to news and current affairs, researched her interviewees, and was thoroughly prepared for her reports. She is always open to opportunities to gain new skills.

Importantly, she makes it a feature of her working practice to operate well within a team. People want to be with other team players who are positive and contribute – which is precisely what Ayu does. She never stagnates – she can't afford to.

Ayu is the consummate professional. Being the best at what she does is part of her philosophy. And that philosophy involves a sense of destiny: "I feel like water, just following a path." But ultimately this is her dream job and she wants to hold on to it.

AYU'S ADVICE

1   Be smart, creative, tough and always learn many things.

2   Keep good relations with everyone.

3   Never doubt yourself.

4   Build up a range of experiences such as internships or freelance work – it also makes your CV look good. Always send your CV in more than once – in case they don't receive it!

5   Every job – however small, big, important or not – try to do it with all your heart. Love your job. Because what we are is what we do in our life.

6   If you don't make any progress, just remember: Never give up! Learn through your mistakes.

COUNTDOWN TO YOUR DREAM JOB
Carole Ann's career coaching boot camp

COMPELLING CLARITY

Immersing themselves in their dream is the driving force of the storytellers in this chapter. Do you think they are lucky to have such a compelling vision? Is your goal attractive enough for you? It is true that when we are passionate about something we are drawn towards it like wasps to the honeypot, and if our dream is clear and irresistible it adds meaning to all the work and searching we put in to find it.

If you feel you are losing sight of your goal, then it is time to redraw your vision and immerse yourself in it in any way you can. Start to tell people what it is you are looking for, ask for favours and imagine yourself already in the new role you seek. What does it feel like, what do you look like, what is life like when you get there?

Hold your dream delicately but firmly, as though holding a small bird in your hand, but still remain focused in the here and now and enjoy life. Don't let your goal dominate every waking hour. Sometimes when we are "pushing" so hard, our expectations primed, our hopes ready at all times for our big break or the phone to ring, it can make the process stressful and we may miss opportunities that don't get past our tunnel vision.

How can you make this process easier and more effortless for yourself?

CAROLE ANN'S ACTION PLAN

1. Offer to do stuff for free in your new chosen profession. Give free taster sessions, workshops, fulfil public speaking appointments – anything you can think of to spread the word about your new passion, possibly attract business by it and explore the waters without investing everything.

2 Network with others who do or want to do what you do.

3 Start a community of like-minders or people who you could share with.

4 Join an e-community of folk who share their expertise – people who work from home have often built e-communities and can recommend accountants, consultants, web designers, PC doctors, etc. There's no need to feel isolated.

5 Share your news. You never know who can help or who may need your services.

6 Get good sound business advice from your bank or accountant. Creative ideas alone do not pay the bills.

7 If you feel you are standing at the edge of the abyss of fear, either placate or torture yourself by telling yourself that the rest of your life could be just as it is right now – making you feel bored, unfulfilled, resentful, undervalued – if you don't jump. Not much of a comfort zone, is it?

8 Accept that it is perfectly OK to feel daunted, scared, apprehensive and fearful. This is exciting stuff and your courage and passion will pay off. Don't lose your nerve.

CHAPTER **9**

MAKING A SUCCESSFUL TRANSITION

" The whole point of being clever, dynamic and motivated is that you get a job you enjoy so that you enjoy your whole life – so that life doesn't start at 6 o'clock in the evening. **"**

Victoria Wood[1]

If the journey thus far has been an exhausting and difficult one, you could well be wondering whether it has all been worth it. You can, of course, opt to stay in the misery you know (the familiar). Or you can reach for your dreams and all the joy and personal satisfaction that they will bring (the unknown).

All transitions come with a loss. We leave behind the familiar and embark on the unknown. Along with the thrills and excitement of the new come anxiety and regret, of course. As human beings we are hard wired to fear change, but pretty soon the unfamiliar becomes as routine as riding a bike. We just need some time and patience with ourselves as we take on these new challenges. Don't lose sight of why it is you are doing all this. Don't forget what your intention was when you set out – and that you have a choice all along the line. You haven't forgotten what you might gain in all this, have you?

Many of the stories in this book show interviewees reaching a "crisis" point. But is that the only way to do it? Is it entirely necessary to reach the point where fear of the day-to-day tedium becomes greater than the fear of change? Do you have to wait for total pain to be your spur? Couldn't the spur be the thrill of the unknown?

Be practical. What freelance work, contracts and appointments can you generate to help convince you that now is the right time to make the move? Building up contacts and knowledge can build confidence. That much-hoped-for career change becomes less scary. Suddenly you're just doing it, rather than dreading it and wondering what it will be like. It's being *in* the swimming pool, rather than that moment before, when you are anticipating plunging into cold water. Start to imagine yourself in this new place. Amaze yourself with what you can get started, what you can find out, who you can meet. Give yourself the chance to surprise yourself – and everyone else – with what you can achieve.

 TOP TIP Decide to make the journey easy and effortless. Unhook from the struggle.

Andy knew nothing about, and no one in, the industry he wanted to work in. But he managed to make the transition from that state of ignorance to the wonderful position of being a respected expert in his chosen field and, most importantly, earning his living in his dream job.

✳ DREAM JOBBER

Andy

Age: 43

Was: Internal auditor, UK

Now: Freelance food writer, UK

Key to success: "The realization that an interested amateur can have as much knowledge and expertise as a professional"

Passion: Food

Andy was introduced to me as someone in the process of making the transition from office job to dream job. He is down to earth, humble, even introverted. He didn't have the advantage of well-connected parents and media contacts in journalism to pave the way for him. He is ordinary. Yet he broke into an extremely competitive field and he did it in ways achievable by all of us.

Andy was trapped in a dispiriting and pressurized job as an internal auditor, but on the sidelines he was pursing his real enthusiasm. His extra-curricular projects enabled him, eventually, to transfer to his dream job. He is someone who made a near-perfect transition. Nevertheless, it took *twenty* years before he felt able to make the change!

After various attempts, he finally took the plunge, left his office job and is now a successful freelance food writer working for national newspapers and magazines in the UK and internationally.

Picture the scene: three people in a half-converted telephone exchange. No windows apart from a narrow skylight, no facilities and barbed wire around the perimeter fence. What could lower your spirits more first thing in the morning?

Can you match that?

Unhappy from day one, why did Andy stay in his job for twenty years? Like many of us, he had commitments. "I needed to pay the mortgage and feed the kids. I couldn't see a way out," says Andy. "I never got ahead, or achieved in my job, because I never enjoyed it." He continued on the treadmill, and while he attempted to leave on numerous occasions he never managed to pull it off.

So how did Andy end up in a job he didn't like in the first place? At seventeen, he needed to get a job in order to leave home. His real enthusiasm at this stage was music and he performed in bands. But he had no idea how to make a career as a musician a reality and he needed money quickly. As a result he applied for a job at a phone company, which he saw advertised in Portsmouth's jobcentre. Twenty years later he was still there.

In his newly acquired bedsit, he ate food that involved adding hot water and stirring. But when his girlfriend came round, he would cook, and his enthusiasm for food grew. (He came from a family where his mother hated cooking and where food was not important, so he was learning from scratch.) London was just beginning to explode with restaurants and Andy would make a significant effort to travel from Portsmouth to visit them. Eating out became a growing passion.

Later he saw an article in his wife's *Elle* magazine. It featured Terence Conran's newly launched London restaurant, Pont de la Tour. For his birthday Andy booked a table, and he describes it as "the pivotal moment that sparked it all off". He's still got the receipt from that meal.

> I was enraptured by it. I looked at it in the magazine and just thought I have to go to this place! It wasn't just the food; when I got there I saw the kitchen's swing doors and I wanted to know what went on behind them. Celebrity chefs were just beginning and I was hugely intrigued and inspired by Marco Pierre White and Gary Rhodes. I wanted to be Pierre White. I had never been a high achiever at work because I wasn't that engaged or interested and in my professional life I had no creativity. I was convinced that being a chef was a creative job.

Andy was so "blown away" by the experience of eating at Pont de la Tour, he wrote a letter to the owner. He said he had been very impressed by his visit and as someone thinking about changing his career, did he have any useful advice? He sent it "FAO Terence Conran". The head chef contacted him and invited him to come and have a look around the kitchens. He then phoned Andy and said he was short staffed on Saturday!

Andy told him that he had no kitchen experience and that he would be of little or no use. But the chef was undeterred. Andy subsequently learnt that all kitchens are short staffed. Every kitchen can use an extra pair of hard-working hands, however untrained. Armed with this knowledge and his newly acquired kitchen experience at Pont de la Tour, Andy felt encouraged to contact other restaurants and request more work experience. Some restaurants said "no", but most said "yes". The plan was to train as a chef, leave the day job and live happily ever after.

That dream ended when his plan to buy a house in London fell through, taking all his savings with it. He and his wife had to reassess and felt that this was no longer the right time. So the office job continued. When he could, Andy ingeniously combined his job with his passion and, when on work trips abroad, he secured work experience in foreign restaurant kitchens. In addition, his job as an auditor trained him in interviewing, fact-checking and report-writing. It required thoroughness and an eye for detail. It equipped him, in hindsight, with highly transferable skills as a journalist.

With his rapidly increasing cooking experience, both at home and in kitchens, Andy entered the BBC's *Masterchef* competition. He was pretty successful – he reached the semi-finals. But, much more importantly, he changed his mind about wanting to be a chef.

> In reality, when I tried it I saw that it *wasn't* creative. Being a chef was a tough grind and often tedious. In hindsight, I'm glad that my plan to leave my job and be a chef didn't work out.

Andy began to reflect and think of other roles he could play within the restaurant industry. He wrote an article about participating in *Masterchef* but he couldn't get it accepted. So he set up his own website, where he would write about food. It was an early form of blog.

> As a result of that venture, I was approached by the food website eGullet.org to become a site moderator for them. Because chefs and food writers look at that website, I began to get known – and to know other people within the industry.

He was making inroads into this "other world" of food. He had been building up a bank of relevant experience. But how could he totally immerse himself in the food world?

Despite being an unsalaried position, Andy's role as eGullet.org moderator paid unexpected dividends. A lunch for site members organized by Andy at the now world-famous Fat Duck restaurant was attended by a leading London restaurant critic who generously agreed to pass on contact details for a number of the UK's top restaurant PR firms. Registering with the companies gave Andy the same access to restaurant events and openings as the food-writing "inner circle".

> Even though an introvert, I wanted to attend these events and talk food with anyone. I am not confident in general, but when talking about food, I am confident enough. In fact, if you like talking about food, you're OK; if you don't, you will find me a crashing bore.

It was simply by continuing to mix in "food" circles that Andy was now attending the same events as the movers and shakers in the food-writing industry. I like the fact that in the early stages Andy initiated food events for the like-minded to come to. It enabled him to explore this other "food" world and share his passion. Setting up and attending these events eventually led to a breakthrough. At one of the PR events he met two editors who would prove instrumental in his career and provide the opportunities for future commissions.

Meanwhile, back at the day job, an opportunity for voluntary redundancy came up which had never been offered before.

By the time this happened, Andy says,

> I had reached a stage where I felt confident that I could make some sort of living before the money ran out. In hindsight it does seem rash, but at the time I didn't feel brave. It was very difficult to get out of internal audit, and I had a long-term boss who wanted people to stay. I knew I would regret it if I didn't do this, but I had no plan beyond my first article.

During those early days in his new career, Andy admits he needed to convince himself that he was a writer. He bought himself a thesaurus, *The Elements of Style* by William Stunk, Jnr, and E. B. White, and Stephen King's book *On Writing*. In addition, he joined the Guild of Food Writers. He had written for some industry magazines for some months, but other than that his only qualifications for writing are his two O levels and memories of an English teacher who clearly saw his potential.

So what made him think he could write and survive in such a competitive field?

> That's a very good question, and the answer is I don't know, except that people seem to like what I write. As an enthusiastic amateur I have learnt that you can compete with the professionals. If you can write, if you know your subject, meet deadlines and are enthusiastic, you can be valuable to editors and make a living. It's surprising to discover there are some in the field who don't write well and don't know their subject. I suspect this applies to other fields. I felt I was the new kid on the block, but actually I knew my stuff as well as others. I had ten years' in-depth experience of cooking and restaurants.

Andy's first year's earnings were shockingly low when set beside the regular income he had been used to. But the commissions are now coming in. He is doing more writing than pitching and, while it's been hard, he doesn't have the daily dread of working that he's had for twenty years. He does struggle with confidence on "off days", and he always feels he should be doing more. "But that's the curse of the freelancer."

He feels his transition is ongoing. He is only just setting up an office and adjusting to being self-employed. But he feels that he made the change well. His only real mistake was to hire office space: it proved to be unnecessary, and expensive.

Andy has succeeded because he knows his stuff, he can write and he meets deadlines. These are key talents, but, equally important, he has been meeting people to whom he can sell his ideas. He took advantage of a redundancy package, because he knew immediately that this was his chance, but in reality he'd been working towards his new job for ten years.

ANDY'S ADVICE

1   Make your transition as soon as possible. Be realistic about what you can afford to live on. I was held back for years by my unwillingness to give up certain luxuries and freedoms. As long as you can feed and house yourself, then do it.

2   When people used to say to me, "Life is not a rehearsal," I would think, Oh, shut up, but now I see that it is so true. I felt trapped, but I was lazy and complacent too, and I regret that. I could have been much more established by now had I left earlier. Deep down, you do know.

3   If you're trying to change career, set up something. If it's music, work in a studio at weekends, make the coffee, meet people. If

you don't know what it is, you need to. Use a "what if" approach; don't limit your horizons. If you have a burning desire for something, you will find the courage and conviction to follow it through.

Andy took twenty years to make his near-perfect career transition. What if you're hoping to do it more quickly and perhaps more than once?

Jennifer has made three major career transitions in her life, and each one in a different country. Her positive and receptive approach to life has led her in all sorts of rewarding directions. "My faith has been restored," she says, "every time I have tried something new." Here's her story …

✳ DREAM JOBBER

Jennifer

Age: 48

Was: Capitol Hill legislative aide, Washington, DC

Now: Managing director, financial PR company, South Africa

Key to success: Being open to opportunity

Passions: Books, people, having a go

To guide her on a daily basis, but also during life-changing decision-making, Jennifer resorts to her gut instinct. She is a firm believer in it and thinks people should use it more often. She has used it throughout her life to build her rewarding but, as she describes it, "dog-legged" career.

When I talk to her over the phone at her home in South Africa, Jennifer comes across as very pragmatic. "What have you got to lose?" she asks herself, each time she applies for a job or gives something a whirl. She isn't fazed by the prospect of rejection. She asked her husband to marry her (she says she was never going to take "no" for an answer), again going on her instinct that he was right for her.

Fundamental to Jennifer is her openness to opportunities that come her way. She's the type of person who is much more likely to say "yes" than "no thanks". That's been key to her career. And because of her agreeable approach to life, people want to work with her.

Jennifer is American, and the story of her career begins on Washington's Capitol Hill, where she worked as a civil servant. Had she always dreamt of getting into politics?

> I lived in a house full of politics, and after doing a fine arts degree I realized you needed lots of new ideas to be able to make it in fine art, and that wasn't me. I went into politics instead, but it didn't feel like a calling, I was just brought up with it. Capitol Hill is run by 23-year-olds, and I was one of those 23-year-olds. There was an opportunity to meet, bond and make a difference. We spent life attending receptions, living off canapés and whisky, but I called for someone to "please kill me if I'm 35 and still here".

> I spent four years in the congressman's office and then two for the governor. After the governor's term expired I applied for a lobbying position with the American College of Surgeons. I came close – after twelve interviews – but a surgeon got the job.

Narrowly missing out on this job proved revelatory and, while she could have slumped into feelings of bitterness and disappointment, Jennifer had a feeling of liberation.

I did feel that the best person won. I was asked a lot in the interviews about why I didn't have a postgrad in public administration. Letters after your name were becoming increasingly important as America became more bureaucratic. It didn't make sense to me. I realized I didn't care that much about the job, and being rejected became less personal. I'm not religious, but I believe in the idea that "God shuts a door and opens a window". Capitol Hill was exciting and meaningful, but also repetitive and labyrinthine. I realized I'd reached a stage where I didn't think I could weather yet another round of budget and appropriations hearings.

Jennifer used this job rejection as an opportunity to pursue her real passion – reading.

I spent my life reading (my mother used to have to throw me outside to play). Even while working in the governor's office, I would read the book reviews before I turned to the politics pages of the newspapers. So after not getting the lobbying job I decided to go to work in a bookstore for $3.75 an hour to see if I liked it. It was a small independent and I was exposed to all aspects of the work of a bookseller. And yes, I absolutely loved it!

She stayed on at the bookshop for two years, and then one of her colleagues asked her to join her in setting up an independent bookshop of their own. Jennifer, always open to opportunities, accepted in spite of not having a clue about starting up a business of this kind.

We began to look around for premises. In the same week we saw an advertisement for Washington DC's oldest general bookstore, which was up for sale. How's that for synchronicity? The bookstore, the Francis Scott Key Bookshop, was in an old (very old) corner townhouse which came with two apartments. So it was all decrepit and dusty and lovely and perfect. I thought I'd die there, an old, decrepit, dusty woman. But there were lots of rich interested buyers. We worked out early on that the executor of the estate wanted to preserve the legacy of the bookshop. It had been run by four chain-smoking women and the place was peeling paint externally and yellowing inside. We could guarantee that we wouldn't change it. After all, we had no money! So, being poor helped in this instance. We also wanted to be hands-on booksellers – unlike other buyers, who would employ others to do it. The seller didn't want maple bookshelves like every other bookstore, she wanted nothing to change. After numerous meetings we knew we really wanted this. Vivian and I sat down and wrote an impassioned letter to the executor to show her how much we wanted it and with our last $5 we got a taxi and shoved the letter under her hotel door. The following day the executor rang and said we could have it.

Pure passion won the owner over and beat off the competition. They researched exactly what the executor was looking for – and they knew they were perfect for the bookshop.

Vivian had inherited a little money, I maxed out my credit cards and between us we managed to cobble together the *exact* amount required to buy Washington DC's oldest general bookstore from the estate of its recently deceased owner of 75 years (how's that for "meant to be"?).

But they not only had the challenge of winning over the executor, they also needed to impress the bookshop's loyal customers.

This proved quite an ordeal, as the locals saw us as interlopers. The neighbourhood loved this bookshop. They considered it theirs and they were deeply suspicious of us taking it over. Emissaries were sent in to test us out. But every time we were quizzed on latest publications, book suggestions, Anthony Powell titles, we passed and eventually got accepted. The bookshop was like something out of Nancy Mitford. People would send their drivers round to pick up books we recommended. Katharine Graham [of the *Washington Post*] would come in looking for books for herself and her grandchildren. Diplomats and ancient men who collected books on spying would be fighting over new releases. We read the obituaries and worked out how much money we'd lose when a regular customer passed away! Eccentrics would come in. We had a customer with the world's pre-eminent Molière collection who used to joke that Yale University was waiting for him to die – he owned two apartments, one for him and one for his books. He owned a signed letter from George Washington. We had no cash register and people bought on account. Only once in five years did someone not pay up.

But how did this major transition to the old-fashioned, quirky world of bookselling really compare to a life in politics?

Choosing a book and making a difference to someone's personal life meant much more to me than assigning a budget. For example, one customer came in looking for books for her holiday. She wanted six and would take anything I gave her. So I went off and thought about it and gave her what I thought would work. I waited and waited for the woman to reappear with her response to what I'd chosen. Eventually she re-emerged to say, "I loved everything you gave me." That meant more to me than the letter of thanks I received from Nancy Reagan! But I would get pangs for politics. I'd see the lights on Capitol Hill indicating a late-night session and I'd have to ask the cab driver to inform me about what was going on. In Washington you are subsumed by the politics.

Jennifer and Vivian lived in the flats that came with the shop and they paid themselves a paltry salary. Jennifer's friends on Capitol Hill, meanwhile, were beginning to make money and would subsidize her meagre pay with meals out.

The downside of bookselling was that it was only barely profitable. I suspect that over time the bigger booksellers of the world would have shut us down. We were also fairly determined only to sell "good books" and were fortunate enough to have a literary community with money. Had we been required to compete commercially, we would have failed.

But Jennifer enjoyed being an unusual bookshop owner in a town dominated by politics. She stood out. And in Vivian she found the perfect partner.

> A new book would come in and she would go away and come back twelve hours later and say, "Take tomorrow off and read it." I was reading six to seven books a week. The Francis Scott Key was renowned for putting books on the map. We often had launch parties in smart Georgetown houses and could sell a couple of thousand copies of someone's son's, or colleague's, or protégé's books. We made friends with the caterers and got quietly drunk in the corner. We once sat under a Renoir just staring at it, knowing we'd never see it again. I felt I was coming into my own. I was getting invited to places. I was unusual – a commodity – in a city dominated by politics. I was enjoying myself and I was sure I would never get married.

Jennifer had her dream job. She felt fulfilled. She felt confident about herself. But, just as she was settling into spinsterhood, one of the bookshop's customers invited her to a party and "the man who opened the door to admit me went on to be my husband". It took just 45 days and her gut instinct to know that this was it. He lived in South Africa, so a long-distance relationship got under way. When they finally married nearly three years later, they'd seen each other for only 45 days in total.

Their correspondence resulted in Jennifer going to South Africa and meeting Tim's family. Politics began to re-emerge as an important element in her life.

> At that time the ANC and South Africa were a big mess. It was the biggest story in the world and Tim was a journalist there and I couldn't take him away from that. I invited him to meet my parents, which proved a very emotional and intense day. There was no warm-up for my parents and I introduced him as the man I was going to marry and live with in South Africa. The conversation moved

quickly from "So, do you have any brothers and sisters?" to "What will you do to protect our daughter if your country blows up?" Tim was grilled by my father: "Jennifer has a huge support group. You're going to have to be all of those people to her." I assured them he would be.

The bookshop continued, but, as it turned out, the landlord needed to sell the building, which contained both the bookshop and the apartments in which Jennifer and Vivian were living. They decided to try to sell the bookshop as a going concern, but couldn't. Eventually it had to be closed down.

Jennifer embarked upon a new phase in her life. When South Africa became a democracy, she left America, her friends and family to join Tim. She had to make the transition from bookshop owner in America to job-hunter in a new country.

When I finally arrived in Cape Town with two cats, my beloved old iron bedstead and 53 boxes of books (poor Tim, he's become an expert at shelf-building), I thought I'd go back to politics because I could never duplicate the most perfect bookstore experience in the world. I didn't want to tarnish the memory. Also, on a practical level in South Africa there was massive illiteracy. So, I wrote to all the political parties offering my services as a researcher. The ANC never wrote back but their opposition did – which was a difficult dilemma to start with. They wanted a paragraph on the ANC's "incoherent foreign policy in Nigeria", about which I knew nothing. It took me seven hours to write that paragraph but I proved to myself that I could do this. It was a crash course in South African politics, and they asked me to write speeches for parliament. "Why speeches?" I asked them. "You've heard a lot of good ones," they replied. And I had. The way I tackled it was to always think about the audience and what they wanted to hear.

After a year, Tim was appointed foreign correspondent in London. Having always wanted to live there, Jennifer happily went with him. As always, she embraced the change and made the transition from political speech-writer in South Africa to job-hunter in London. So what this time? When a friend pointed out an advert for an assistant literary agent, Jennifer applied. Where does the courage and self-belief come from? I asked her.

> Well, what have you got to lose? Really, what is the worst that can happen? Whenever I have taken a leap of faith I have been rewarded every time. I was open to a life change. I wanted to work in London. There was no point in regretting the end of the bookstore or regretting leaving South Africa. I do believe if you are open to the universe you will be rewarded for being receptive to it. My faith has been restored every time I have tried something new.

The agent appointed Jennifer as her literary assistant. During the twenty months she was employed there, Jennifer was able to "get back on the couch with manuscripts and snacks from where I vetted about a thousand and got three accepted by publishers".

She left this job when she returned to South Africa and another career decision loomed. The independence she'd experienced at the agency led Jennifer to think about setting up something freelance.

> At this point I decided I wanted to work from home. I got a gig or two lined up (one to make journalism out of a friend's think-tank research and the other to read manuscripts for a publisher) and needed one more to make a decent living. I ran into an acquaintance at a bar. He offered me some work while one of his colleagues went on maternity leave. They subsequently landed a big client in the asset management industry and I started work (full time) the next day.

I pointed out to Jennifer that it hadn't taken much for her to leave her freelancing "game plan" behind (well, a couple of drinks!). But from her point of view, an opportunity had come her way and, as ever, she was amenable to it.

> The job was advising corporate and quasi-governmental organizations (the Competition Commission, for instance) about their media and investor relations. The person who appointed me could see that, although I knew nothing about business (or media relations), I could learn. Some of the CEOs I have advised still know more about PR than I do. In theory it was only for four months' maternity cover and then they would parcel work out to me. But then the company got bigger and they needed somebody for longer than that. It was another opportunity and I thought "why not?"

> My husband says he notes an innate confidence in Americans. He says he detects a belief that they can be anything they want to be if they try. It may be true. But with this job I simply felt I had done elements of the PR job before. I had sold manuscripts and I knew I could sell a story. I had absolutely no training in people management – but there seem to be fewer people leaving the company! The financial stuff was also completely new to me, but naturally exciting. The biggest challenge has been not losing heart looking up at steep "learning curves".

Nearly nine years on, and Jennifer still works with the same company.

> I was charged with developing the business (and adding and retaining clients and employees) in Johannesburg. Over the past eight years, we've grown from income of R140,000 per month with eight employees to over a million and a half a month with 27 employees. I'm exhausted just typing that. I found that my dog-legged career path helped my success. Capitol Hill taught me to respect, but not fear, power – so I'm able to appropriately advise CEOs. Selling an 80,000-word book assisted me to "sell" a 700-word story to a reporter. And all that reading, I hope, helped me string a decent sentence together to put together press releases or opinion editorials. While I learnt about managing people on the job (as most do), I should

imagine that empathy learned from reading novels allowed me to successfully tap into people correctly so that I could corral, implore and demonstrate rather than instruct and demand.

On a good day I love the fact that I can rely on my wits and instinct. It's fun because of the people with whom I interact and maintain a sense of irony. It's rewarding *every* day because of what I can make of lessons, challenges – even cranky, angry moments. On a bad day I think I need to retire because this much stress doesn't do a body any good!

But what about all those books she hasn't had time to read? Are there any regrets?

Not a one. In all three of my professions no day was the same. All involved reading and thinking and advising (I guess everyone likes to be paid to have an opinion!) and all allowed me to know fascinating people. South Africa is an amazing place, it's like the USA in the fifties. Entrepreneurship is a way out of poverty. Everyone is behind it and there is moral support for people trying to succeed. If you have the energy and an idea out here you can do anything. People will take a chance on you. I feel privileged to advise smart people about their businesses. I have exposure to amazing brains. It covers advocacy and politics and things like whistle-blowing legislation. I had a good day yesterday when I contributed to exposing collusion in anti-competitive trading among bread companies. Bread is a basic staple over here. It's all over the news today. I sleep better when that happens. As for the books, well, yes, depressingly someone told me recently it would take fifteen years just to read all the *titles* of books I have to get around to reading!

Jennifer wants to retire at 50. "How's it looking?" I asked. That plan is also coming along. They bought some land three years ago before prices rocketed and they have a small cottage on it. So in the background they've got plans on the back burner. They're working towards building a house there with a kitchen garden, and Jennifer looks forward to catching up with all the books she hasn't yet had time to read. Husband Tim has just gone freelance with his job, which gives him a bit more flexibility. But Jennifer and I both agree that she probably won't ever retire. She'll be offered something else that she'll be open to and will be totally rewarded by.

Is Jennifer someone who's just been very fortunate in life? I think she's a great example of someone who isn't born lucky, but has created her own fortune and opportunities. It's clear she's personable, positive and friendly. Because of that, people are drawn to her and want to team up with her.

If there's a choice, who do you want in your line-up? The person who's competent, fun and open to suggestions? Or the person who's competent, negative and wearisome?

I think Jennifer proves you can create your own chances. If you're magnetic, people will want you with them. Are you someone other people want to work with? Jennifer didn't quite know where she was going or what she wanted to do, but she was open to change. If you don't know what you want to do, being open to change is a good start. It could take you *anywhere*.

JENNIFER'S ADVICE

1   For anyone who's feeling stuck in a rut or trapped in the wrong job, be aware of possible doors opening – even if it's just a crack. If you can take some risk financially or emotionally, step through.

2   You're far more likely to regret not taking a chance than taking it (though that same instinct can tell you if an opportunity offered is not right).

What is more regretful: fifteen years unhappy in a job and never trying to make change, or having a go, even if it's a bad move that has to be rectified?

COUNTDOWN TO YOUR DREAM JOB
Carole Ann's career coaching boot camp

Now you could be on the precipice of a wonderful new life, hovering there on the edge. With all your conflicting thoughts, it may be a frightening place. Looking back on the glory stories of the book and the people behind them will show you that these people are not superhuman, nor do they possess extraordinary powers that made their journey smooth and trouble free. They are ordinary people like you who have worried, lost sleep and been as scared of moving on as you are today. They have stood where you are, on the brink of a brave new life, and then they took a deep breath and jumped.

It's worth noting that two common factors among our contributors is that (a) they wished they hadn't worried so much about the leap, and (b) they wished they'd made the move sooner.

Will that be you looking back and saying those very same things one day?

Now might be the time to ask yourself:

> How can I stop struggling with the process of seeking my dream job?
>
> What can I stop doing that's not helping me?
>
> What am I afraid to confront?
>
> How can I simplify what I'm doing?

Be patient: give yourself plenty of time to try new things and for new ideas to work. You have been brave and journeyed the path less travelled; now you're on the final step.

CAROLE ANN'S ACTION PLAN

1. Be open to offers – think "yes" and say "yes" rather than "no thanks". You can think about whether you can do it or want what's on offer later.

2. If you don't know what you want to do, like Jennifer, be open to change – it could take you anywhere. Even doing something for fun rather than money could be a worthwhile step.

3. When setting out in your new career, be prepared to be the best that you can – know your subject, build up experience, meet deadlines, be reliable, and be sure to give yourself time to settle in. You can't know everything immediately.

4. Don't spend unnecessarily on external office space, furniture, gadgets or business cards. A space, a PC and a phone are all you need at the start.

5. When you make the break, tell the world, hold a party and give yourself a big pat on the back. You deserve all the self-praise and applause you can get. Never, ever forget how courageous you have been.

6. Give yourself at least a year to settle into your new path. The phone doesn't ring the second your website goes live, and the creative flow may not immediately gush the second you close the door on your old career. Be gentle on yourself and be prepared for a learning curve.

7. There will be ups and downs, there is no design for life, but don't give up straight away. Be realistic .

CHAPTER **10**

FINDING YOUR
DREAM JOB

“Doing what you're passionate about is the only way to enjoy life.**”**

Clarissa Dickson Wright[1]

We are nearing the end of the book and maybe getting to the end of the journey you have been on to find your dream job too. Or at least a significant step closer to finding out how to get there.

On a fundamental level, you may have reconnected with the possibility that we're put here for a purpose, to live a life that is useful, fulfilled and satisfying. In this role you would live and work according to your values and use the best of your unique abilities to make each working day meaningful.

By anyone's standards, spending years dreading each working day, literally killing time as you waste your health and youth doing something you resent, is no way to fulfil this vision or to live a life.

Some of you may well be up and at 'em, in action, making plans, devising strategies and, perhaps for the first time, seeing a real direction to move in. It's a glimpse worth chasing with all your heart.

If you are well on your way to doing what you love, here are some tips to keep you focused and functioning in your brave new world.

Once you find your dream job, how do you ensure that you don't fall out of love with it?

If things begin to feel a bit humdrum and routine, it's important to recognize that, as with any relationship, there will always be bad hair days, rainy days, dull days – that's life. My penultimate story is an example of how to keep the momentum going when in pursuit of a long-term ambition.

✱ DREAM JOBBER

Vicky

Age: 49

Was: Solicitor, UK

Now: Judge, UK

Key to success: Faith, hard work and knowing her goal

Passions: Stimulating work, social justice

Vicky began as a lawyer. Her goal was to become a circuit judge. In spite of it being a traditional profession, she strove to innovate and introduce variety into her legal work, and this ensured that her engagement with it continuously evolved and developed.

She established for herself a number of roles, all of which made for a full-time job that was worthwhile and rewarding. Having a cluster of different responsibilities is also a good way of combining the elements you enjoy and minimizing time in roles you don't. In addition, all the roles were chosen because they would assist in achieving Vicky's ultimate goal and enable her to perform the job better should she achieve her goal.

Here is the portfolio of jobs that she set up:

- Partner in a firm of solicitors

- Recorder, i.e. part-time judge (sitting in a crown court with a jury)

- Member of the Parole Board for England and Wales (involves meeting long-term prisoners, and deciding if and when it is appropriate to release them)

- Shadow trustee of a UK charity helping people to find and keep work

Vicky has worked her way up through the ranks. It has involved a lot of hard work and there have been no short cuts. Keeping up with the demands of all the different roles was her greatest challenge: "While having this portfolio of jobs ensured my work was fulfilling, the demands were high." But not only did it keep the work varied and interesting, it ensured she continued to broaden her skills and knowledge for her ultimate goal. Whatever your area of work, this is an entirely sensible approach. It means Vicky is informed about the whole legal process, from the sentencing in court to its repercussions for offenders in prison.

She was lucky in that she knew from an early age she wanted to be a judge, and nowadays she loves waking up and realizing what lies ahead.

> Trials are the hardest work, but the most fulfilling. It's complicated work and highly charged. As the judge, I will be on the edge of my seat, ready to step in and make crucial decisions. I have to be in control of the proceedings. It is not until the end when the summing up is done and I have given the final essential instructions to the jury before they retire to reach their verdict that I feel my job is done.

This mentally challenging work was balanced by her desk job as a partner in a firm of solicitors. Vicky found that this was where she could have "down days". "Offices generate their own microclimates," she says, "and you end up getting ground down by what are really trivialities." But responsibility for the employees has been an essential part of her job.

Vicky's background is different from that of most recorders because she hasn't been a barrister. She had to make a tough transition to criminal law. But when the opportunity arose, she demonstrated her resourcefulness. Faced with the challenge of acquiring a thorough knowledge of criminal law, in order to give herself the best chance possible of being able to compete for this job, she organized a "personal trainer".

> I engaged this person to come round for an hour once a week for eight weeks to help me revise criminal law. The day of the interview dawned and, feeling nervous, I made the mistake of striking up a conversation with the candidate next to me. He had *twenty years'* experience of criminal law. I remained nervous and wondered why, exactly, I was putting myself through this.

But in those few moments she remembered a piece of advice she'd been given about telling the panel how she had prepared for the interview. She explained that she had worked with a personal trainer. It was something that hadn't been done before and was well received.

> But there are no short cuts. For that interview I did everything I was meant to do. I took advice from all quarters. Even the night before, when all I wanted to do was relax, I made calls to people who had more advice to offer.

According to a lifelong friend, Vicky's success is down to three things: brilliant people skills; incredible tenacity; and a strong public service ethic. Vicky, on the other hand, feels her success is down to faith, hard work and knowing her goal.

She found working as a solicitor the hardest part of her career. "It's a difficult job. You work under enormous pressures and the focus is off the law and is more about running a business, human resources and public relations." She went on to become a partner in a major international law firm, but it didn't feel worthwhile, so she left.

Vicky firmly believes that there are so many ways in which to earn your living these days that picking what you want to do is a genuine option. But whatever you choose to do, once you get there it's important to ensure that you keep evolving and learning, setting goals and doing whatever you do to the best of your ability. I am pleased to say she has fulfilled her goal and is now a judge.

VICKY'S ADVICE

1   When you're at a low ebb, remember it's temporary, and a good night's sleep is a great starting point to feeling better.

2   Don't just walk out of the job. Grit your teeth – take time off if you need to – but work out what you want to do and then establish how you can get there.

3   Don't be unhappy. Think. And plan.

 That which you resist, persists.

So that's the story of someone who set up a portfolio of jobs to maintain variety in a long-term career plan, and at the same time chose specific roles that would give her the vital experience she needed for her ultimate goal and dream job as a circuit judge.

Geoff is also someone who has been in the same job for a long time. He created his dream job fifteen years ago, and loves it so much he just can't leave. He is someone who genuinely can't wait to get to work each day, and is addicted to his work. He exudes enthusiasm and passion the moment he starts talking about it. It seems fitting, therefore, that he should provide the final story in the book.

✱ DREAM JOBBER

Geoff

Age: 36

Was: Arts management student, UK

Now: Director of the Leicester Comedy Festival, UK

Key to success: Creating a job doing what he is good at

Passion: Organizing

Geoff was an arts management student at the University of Leicester. Inspired by the growing popularity of comedy as "the new rock and roll", the idea of running a comedy festival came up as part of a student project.

> I had two friends who worked loosely in comedy, so I said I'd ring them to talk about it. I don't know why, but I just started to get really excited about it. Everyone else cleared off during the summer holidays, but I stayed and worked on the idea of a festival. And that's how it began. A group of us got some sponsors and set about hiring venues and acts. The first festival was held the following February and had 5,000 visitors. Comedian Harry Hill performed to a room of 25. Now the festival happens every year and attracts over 60,000 people. It's the longest-running comedy festival in Britain. Several years on from that original idea, and I'm still here!

But how did he manage to transform a student project into his livelihood?

> I really enjoyed doing the festival. In my final year I just did that, nothing else, and, as a result, my dissertation was awful! After graduation I needed to decide what I was going to do next. I knew I didn't want to return to working in London and I didn't really have

anything else to do. Here was this festival in Leicester, albeit small, but it worked and was really exciting. I had this thing right in front of me and I suppose I just thought – well, I'm just going to do that. Why not? Why wouldn't you? Even though I still wasn't paid, I was working in bars in the evening to get money, I just don't think I ever had any choice in the matter. I just remember thinking that's what I'm going to do, I'm going to run the festival.

Geoff revels in busy-ness and loves the demands in the run-up to the festival. When the phones stop ringing he struggles. I met him in a café after the festival had finished for another year. He was immediately affable and charismatic. His enthusiasm quickly ignites when he starts to talk about what he does and all the things in the coming year he looks forward to. It's clear he is someone who relishes the challenge of making things happen.

But I think Geoff's real talent is *knowing what his skills are*. He's aware of what he enjoys and what switches him on. He stuck to a job when he created one that thrilled him – in spite of more lucrative offers from other festivals.

In fact, Geoff didn't stumble across his line of work entirely by chance. He has always had a fairly clear idea about what he wanted to do – *organize* something.

I knew from the age of twelve I wanted to be a promoter, although I'm not sure I really knew what that meant! We didn't do work experience at school, but I told my teacher that in order for me to get a good understanding of the music industry, I needed experience. They let me take a week off and work at A&M Records. When I left school I wrote to a record label, and then rang them up when I got no reply. I was taken on even though I was an eighteen-year-old with very little experience; a guy called Richard gave me a chance. I worked for him for a year in London with a pop group who ran their own record label. That was the first group I'd ever promoted. Richard became an inspiration and mentor. I learnt loads about the business from him. Sometimes I find myself doing things and thinking, That's what Richard would have done.

Mentors like Richard are an important factor for many of the interviewees in this book, providing invaluable advice or opportunities to build up some solid work experience. Geoff gained more experience through his student project, and after graduating he simply decided to carry on. No one offered it to him; the festival wasn't going to continue unless he took it on, raised the money and made it happen. It would have been easier in some ways to walk away, but, because he enjoyed doing it, staying on and continuing made sense – to him.

> It's just bizarre, looking back. What people thought, I do not know, but two friends and I just sat in a room in Leicester and carried on doing it. We'd say, "Yep, we're doing the second Leicester festival." We had no money, but after much effort we got sponsorship – and suddenly we had £25,000, which was very exciting *and* scary. It had been a game up to that point. But all of a sudden it was really serious.

I like this idea that it was just a game, they were having fun, following a passion – really not sure where it was headed or whether they could pull it off. But the small team of three had the necessary dedication and determination to succeed, enabling the second festival to happen – and it was better than the first.

The high for Geoff is the ten-day event itself. "I love it when there's a comedian on stage, the layout is right, the auditorium is packed and it's working. I'm enormously proud of what we've done. We have people who take a week off work to come to the festival. We have people who write in saying, this is what I'm looking forward to, it's the best thing in the world." But there are low points – and I've joined Geoff during the main one.

In the run-up to the festival, the number of emails and phone calls you get is huge. You're all working towards something, it's going to happen. Literally the day after, nobody rings you, nobody emails you. There's nothing. But you still have to go in, you still have to work out how many people came, do the invoicing, finance and all that dross. It's really hard and it's the most hideous time for weeks every year after the festival. It's a common ailment among all festival organizers!

Geoff has his dream job. But there are still tedious elements within it. He accepts it as part of the festival cycle. It's during this difficult time, when he is still reeling from the highs and lows of the festival, that Geoff attends an annual meeting to negotiate for money for next year. There is much at stake. If he doesn't get the funding, there is no festival, and he and his colleagues are out of a job. In spite of another bigger and better festival under his belt, he has to start from scratch and convince every person in that room that the festival is worth continuing with. Every year, people say it's not going to happen.

One October we had no money. I've always known that we were going to carry on, but I didn't know how. The festival is a really good thing. You can't not do it, because it's so good. It's like cheating if you don't do it. We had meetings until 3 a.m. looking at bank statements which spelt out that we couldn't afford it. But I'm thinking, We have to do it. Everyone around me is saying "You can't". I don't know how we've achieved it, but we work out a way to do it, and we always have done every year since we started. I don't think many independent festivals have survived every year since 1994. It's really unusual.

The determination to keep going is evident in Geoff from the moment he starts talking. He's upbeat and already thinking of plans for next year's festival. He's enjoying piecing together his narrative; he's never thought about how and why he got here. He had no clear, long-term strategy – he just pursued what he enjoyed and what he felt he was good at. For the time being he seems addicted to the festival, with a conviction that it must take place each year.

Is Geoff in a job for life, or will he make his own career change one day? Can he foresee being stuck in his own rut?

> Somebody once said that festival directors ought to leave every two or three years because they get bored and tired, and you can tell in the programme, because it becomes repetitive and the marketing is dull and boring. But I've been involved with the comedy festival for such a long time in terms of building it up and making it grow, I don't know whether I could leave it and move on. That's quite a difficult thing – at what point do I let go? I've been offered really good jobs for lots more money. But I've not taken them. I often jokingly say I can't do anything else. But I don't think I could. At the moment, I don't want to do anything else. I imagine at some point the opportunity of moving and getting a lot of money for doing very little will mean that I'll leave, but no one's offered me that yet! If we did a festival that wasn't better than last year's, then I'd stop. But so far, it's got better and better. At the moment I can't really imagine *wanting* to be anywhere else or doing anything else. Why would I want to? I absolutely love it.

Repeatedly during my research, people who love their work have talked about the importance of the people they work with. For a happy working environment, getting the right mix is vital, both for the employer and for the employee.

So Geoff makes sure he appoints what he considers to be the right team, and that's another reason why he considers he has the perfect job.

> I have a team of six people at work who inspire me, and they would say the same about me (I hope!). We're all similar types of people. I have total respect for our manager, whose job I could never do, and she says the same about me and my role. But we work together and

complement each other and that's key to getting the right team. I suppose it's our approach. We all go to work because we think it's really good, and not to earn money. We don't have anyone who just comes and does their job and takes their wages and goes home again.

I sense that Geoff's job provides a thrill and interest that expensive holidays and cars can't match. He's used to living without money and he simply isn't prepared to give up what he loves for a salary and a job he's convinced will be less exciting.

> I get everything out of my job that someone who feels stuck and bored in theirs doesn't. But I don't have money. When it started I had enough money to live but didn't have holidays and cars. So I did bar work elsewhere, which became onerous. There was a bit of time when I worked for a venue in Leicestershire for a local authority and I did that partly to get money. At 25 I was fed up with not having any money, as you would be, but I've never had an office job and I don't understand office politics. I don't know what it's like to play games at work. But there is something about the structure and security that appeals to some people. My partner gets in and does nine to six, with an hour for lunch, and likes that routine. I can't understand that and I've never experienced it. I can see myself doing what I'm doing until I'm 50. Same job pretty much for the whole of my life. But I don't want to do anything else! I don't want to earn £50,000 at the expense of everything else.

> My family are glad I do something I enjoy. I think they accept that I'm not going to get a "proper" job. It's just what I do. My dad would prefer me to get a proper job. My mum was a nursery nurse and my dad was in insurance. One of my brothers is an academic and works at Leicester University. My other brother works for a housing association.

All the people I have spoken to for the purposes of this book have found a job that draws on their strengths. How many people are really doing a job that, like Geoff's, draws on what they do best? Geoff, the born organizer, organizes every day of his life. At the very core of what he *does* all day is what he enjoys, what he is good at and what switches him on.

If a job doesn't draw on your skills or enthusiasms and there is nothing in it of you – is it any wonder it's a struggle to enjoy it?

And Geoff has recruited a team of people who have talents he admires. He works with like-minded people and they share a common enthusiasm for making the festival a brilliant, memorable experience. It's another common factor in those who enjoy their work – colleagues are inspirational, like-minded enthusiasts. Geoff is ambitious for the festival – rather than for himself . And so is the team. Their enthusiasm lies in *the work they are doing*. It is that which seems to propel their success over naked personal ambition.

Geoff cannot imagine sticking with a job he doesn't love. "Why would you stay?" he asks. When I asked him, "What would your advice be to someone stuck in a rut?" he replied, "What?" He didn't even understand the question.

GEOFF'S ADVICE

1   Arrange work experience.

2   Take a day off work and shadow someone in a different job.

3   Hunt out an environment where you'll find like-minded people with values that match yours.

4   Try different things until you find something you feel passionate about. Do what you're good at.

SO, IN CONCLUSION

In hindsight, it all sounds so obvious, doesn't it? But we did it – we worked in offices we didn't like in jobs where we were bored out of our boxes. Why, we ask ourselves from shiny new lives, did we put up with it for so long? When we didn't know where we were going, did we look, research, experiment – or did we sit stupefied by the prospect, too appalled by the size of the mountain that lay ahead to even start the journey?

This book is a testament to people overcoming fear, a testament to those daring to reach for their dreams in the belief that there's got to be more. All of the contributors to this book are ordinary, *yet extraordinary*, people – some with families, some with support and some operating alone. They all juggled financial demands and varying reactions from family and friends. None of them was born with luck. They each created it. They could be any one of us.

What do these stories offer someone hoping for change? What conclusion can we draw from them?

My aim has been to demonstrate how things happen. How you can increase the chances of finding the dream job by making contacts, meeting people and competing in a world that at first feels impossible to penetrate. My stories show that change can happen for a variety of people in a variety of ways. Their tactics, their timescales, the number of their job interviews, rejections and helping hands all differ. But those who went out looking for change found change. And no one regretted the decision to go looking.

Some were passive, but open to opportunities. Others went actively looking for their vocation in life. In the process, the fear that had grabbed some of them by the throat and paralysed them for too long fell away. They had hung around worrying and waiting for the "right move". And it was often the *wrong* moves which provided the most useful information. Even those who had no idea where they were going (and many of them are still in the process of finding out) knew that leaving their job was the right thing to do, and don't regret it.

THE TRUTH ABOUT SUCCESSFUL CAREER CHANGE

- If you want change, there is a process that can lead you to where you want to go.
- All types of people make successful change.
- You can create your own luck and opportunities.
- Doors open for those who try.
- Doors open to energized and magnetic people.
- They also open to the shy, hopeful and persistent.
- Some questioned why they let it all drag on to crisis stage before making a move.
- It was scary, but not as scary as imagined.
- Change, however small, provides new perspectives and information.
- Investigation brings about hope, energy, new leads, opens doors and provides direction by closing others.
- Trying new things out enabled my interviewees to learn new things about themselves – both their strengths and their weaknesses.
- Most experienced a phase of "I'm not getting anywhere". Stopping the struggle and enjoying the process was vital to keeping going.

- It always takes longer than you imagine.

- No one regretted having tried to make change. They only regretted not having done it sooner.

- In every case, it led to something better.

COUNTDOWN TO YOUR DREAM JOB
Carole Ann's career coaching boot camp

SO WHAT WOULD YOU LIKE YOUR LEGACY TO BE?

Surrounded by your great-grandchildren, do you want to say, "Oh, I didn't do what I wanted to because I was too scared to change. But at least I met my mortgage payments," or "I followed my dream and you must too"?

What would you like people to say about your life? What do you want to say about it?

Life goes by in the blink of an eye. Where did the last five years go? Can you remember what you did, what you achieved in those past 1,825 days? If you have come this far in the book and are still feeling fed up, envious, fatigued, depressed, drained and lost, then make these feelings your wake-up call.

VISION MAKING

This is the last coaching exercise in *Find Your Dream Job*. It is powerful, exciting and revealing. If you still don't know what it is you are looking for, this exercise is for you.

Really give yourself permission to dream big here and have fun with it. Be as descriptive and creative as possible. Write down your vision, find pictures and put them somewhere you can see them every day. Let them guide you and inspire you into action.

The Big Dream Interview

It is five years from now and a journalist from your favourite newspaper or magazine is coming to interview you about something you've done – your successes.

They are walking to your home.

What does it look like, where is it?

How is the garden looking? Where is it located? By the sea, overlooking Sydney Harbour? In a Philippe Starck-designed apartment block? A Cotswolds cottage? A Barcelona studio? A ski lodge? Describe your dream home.

You open the front door. How do you look? Toned, suntanned, healthy, slimmer, relaxed? What are you wearing? Cashmere, jeans, a business suit, workout gear, diamonds? Pile on the detail. Describe the interior of the house – what does the journalist see? Think big and add smells, sounds, colours, textures, light, windows. Be as creative as you want – this is your dream, your mind's eye, so give yourself permission to allow abundance. Are those orchids in a vase? Can you smell fresh coffee? Is it time for a glass of champagne?

Are there other people there? Housekeepers, nanny, secretary, partner, children, house guests, relatives, pets?

Do you have an office? What's in it? State-of-the-art or traditional?

Are there any sounds you are hearing? Birds, horses, the buzz of the city, the sea? Immerse yourself in the dream. Is someone playing the piano somewhere? Is your latest interview playing on a flat-screen TV? The journalist would be taking all this in and adding it to the feature for a true colour piece.

Do you have any other homes? Where are they? How does this home reflect the you you've become?

Now pay attention.

The journalist asks you to give her readers a piece of advice that you would give someone who is currently down, confused and fed up and doesn't know which way to turn – just as you were five years ago. What do you say? Write it down, bold and bright.

This is the advice your higher self (the person you are when fear is not in control and you allow your true brilliance to flourish) is giving to you today to get you there! Are you going to follow it?

Really enjoy this task – it's your dream, you can make it as wonderful as possible, as lavish, as eccentric and as wild as you like. Feel your heart sing, see it soar and, just for now, don't ask "how?"

Good luck, and may the first step be today.

NOTES

CHAPTER 1: THE RUT

1   *The Observer*, "The 50 Men who understand Women", 11 February 2007.

2   *Daily Mirror*, reporting a survey by Learn Direct, the not-for-profit careers and skills organization, 30 August 2007.

3   Alex Jones, "About Time for Change", Work Foundation, 2003, cited in Madeleine Bunting's *Willing Slaves*, June 2004, p. 28.

CHAPTER 2: A MENTAL SHIFT TO THE NEW YOU

1   *Imagine: The Secret of Life*, BBC1, 19 February 2008.

CHAPTER 3: IDENTIFYING AND GETTING OVER OBSTACLES

1   *J. K. Rowling: A Year in the Life – Putting Potter to Bed*, ITV, 30 December 2007.

2   YouGov survey of 2,500 lawyers for *The Lawyer* magazine, 2 July 2007.

CHAPTER 4: WHAT IS IT YOU WANT? WHAT ARE YOUR VALUES?

1   Stanford Report, 12 June 2005. Full text available at http://news-service.stanford.edu/news/2005/june15/grad-061505.html.

CHAPTER 5: ACTION IS ALL

1   Lucy Cavendish, "The very colourful life of our fabric queen", *Evening Standard*, 16 October 2006.

CHAPTER 6: REFLECTION

1   Quoted by "dream jobber" Tanya, from the film *A Touch of Infidelity*.

CHAPTER 7: RESTRUCTURING

1 Lynn Barber, "Let him eat cake", *Observer*, 25 May 2008.

CHAPTER 8: IMMERSION

1 Antoinette Odoi, "Tis the season to be thinking of a new job", *Observer*, 13 January 2008.

CHAPTER 9: MAKING A SUCCESSFUL TRANSITION

1 *The Apprentice: You're Fired* (series 4, episode 12), BBC2, 11 June 2008.

CHAPTER 10: FINDING YOUR DREAM JOB

1 Tom Templeton, "Introducing ... Thomasina Miers", *Observer*, 30 October 2005.

FURTHER READING

Martha Beck, *Finding Your Own North Star: How to claim the life you were meant to live* (Piatkus, 2001)

Martha Beck, *The Joy Diet: 10 steps to a happier life* (Piatkus, 2003)

Po Bronson, *What Should I Do With My Life?: The true story of people who answered the ultimate question* (Vintage, 2004)

Guy Browning, *Office Politics: How work really works* (Ebury Press, 2006)

Tom Hodgkinson, *How to Be Idle* (Penguin, 2005)

Tom Hodgkinson, *How to Be Free* (Penguin, 2007)

Herminia Ibarra, *Working Identity: Unconventional strategies for reinventing your career* (Harvard Business School Press, 2003)

Oliver James, *Affluenza* (Vermilion, 2007)

Carmel McConnell, *Soultrader: Find purpose and you'll find success* (Pearson Education, 2002)

Christopher J. A. Smith, *"Why Don't You Fly?": Back door to Beijing – by bicycle* (Pen Press, 2005). See also www.cycleuktochina.com

Tessa Souter, *Anything I Can Do … You Can Do Better: How to unlock your creative dreams and change your life* (Vermilion, 2006)

Polly Toynbee, *Hard Work: Life in low-pay Britain* (Bloomsbury, 2003)

ABOUT THE AUTHORS

SARAH WADE

After waitressing, cleaning men's toilets and a stint emptying cardboard boxes, Sarah took a job as a TEFL teacher in former Czechoslovakia, which led her to listen to the BBC World Service. This set her on a path to a career in radio back in the UK. Now a BBC producer, she has interviewed comedians, writers, politicians and people with fascinating stories to tell. Recently this has spilled over into a spare-time obsession with talking to and interviewing ordinary people who have made extraordinary efforts to find jobs they love. This personal passion has led to Sarah writing her first book.

CAROLE ANN RICE

Carole Ann started out wanting to be an artist, but instead became a waitress and door-to-door salesperson, and once operated the tail end of a snail in a TV puppet show instead. "Having your hand up a snail's derrière all day is a wake-up call. I know too well the agony of the dead-end job," she recalls.

Now she has found her own dream job as a coach.

She is also an award-winning journalist and one-time TV presenter/programme-maker for BBC and ITV. She has written for the *Independent on Sunday*, the *Sun*, the *Birmingham Post*, the *Daily Express*, *She* and *Red* magazine. Her clients include the London School of Economics, Visa and Marks and Spencer.

She lives a happy life in London with her husband, a political commentator, and their two children.

Sarah and Carole Ann would love to know how you get on in your mission, and can be contacted via their websites: www.findyourdreamjob.co.uk and www.realcoachingco.com.

ACKNOWLEDGEMENTS

Huge thanks to everyone who agreed to contribute to my research and to all who helped on this book: Neil, Carole Ann, Andrew, Jenny King, Andy Milligan, Martin Liu, John Simmons, Pom Somkabcharti, David Chapman, Paul Forty, Trudie Treasure, Dawn, Elaine and all at the Carry On Club.